JOHN PAUL II
THE POPE FROM POLAND

Joannes Paulus pp II

JOHN PAUL II
THE POPE FROM POLAND

Second enlarged edition

Tadeusz Karolak

Interpress Publishers • Warsaw 1979

Translated by
David Evans

Designed by
Jerzy Kępkiewicz

ISBN 83-223-1845-6

"And so the most reverend cardinals have appointed a new Bishop of Rome. They have summoned him from a far distant country but one which has always been close in the community of faith and the Christian tradition."

From the first address of greeting to the crowd by the newly elected Pope, John Paul II (16 October 1978)

On 16 October 1978, a few minutes after 6 p.m., a new pope was elected by the College of Cardinals on the second day of the Conclave. The election was announced to the crowds gathered in St. Peter's Square by Cardinal Pericle Felici according to the traditional formula: Nuntio vobis gaudium magnum: Habemus papam *(I announce to you a great joy: we have a pope)*. He announced that the new pope was Cardinal Karol Wojtyła who had taken the name of John Paul II.

This is how the pontificate of the new Pope, the first Pope from Poland, began. The world news media broadcast the amazing announcement and within seconds people began to talk about the Cardinal from far-away Cracow and to look on the map for foreign-sounding place-names – Wadowice, Lublin, Częstochowa – and everywhere people were talking about Poland.

Cardinal Karol Wojtyła, Archbishop of Cracow, was already well-known in Poland. He was so well-known in fact that really the Poles knew little about him apart from some general facts, and it was not until his name came to be known all over the world, until reporters began to trace almost his every step from birth, that they saw how interesting and rich his life had been.

5

To try and write about the first 58 years of the life of Karol Wojtyła is not an easy task even though this chapter has already come to an end. There has not yet been an appropriate lapse of time to observe certain facts in their true light. On the other hand the Archbishop of Cracow has led such a rich and intensive life that more time is required to gather together all the events in which he took part or of which he was the main instigator. This outline is really a straightforward attempt at writing about a life which cannot be presented in detail in a few pages. The problem is still greater for even basic facts about the personal life of Karol Wojtyła are inextricably bound up with facts about the life of the community. This was particularly the case when as bishop, archbishop, and cardinal, he administered the Cracow archdiocese, or as Professor of the Catholic University of Lublin, author of widely-read books, member of the Second Vatican Council or as a member of the Polish episcopate, he participated in the spiritual and intellectual life of many sections of the community. In reality it is very difficult to divide the later period of Karol Wojtyła's life into what was exclusively his own preserve and what he did for others. All of this merges into one and is one of the characteristics of a biography of the Cardinal from Cracow. Another characteristic is his gift for gathering people around him. Innumerable people look upon him as a friend and Cardinal Wojtyła acquired friends in all walks of life and, what is more important, he never forgot these people, not even amid the overwhelming demands of his work and activities. He was always available. He was open to dialogue, just like the Church in the period after the Second Vatican Council.

If anyone wishes to know what sort of man he was, how those who have met him remember him, where he lived and what sort of environment he was brought up and educated in, how he grew up, and what he brought or gave to others, to all of these questions and others I shall try and give an answer by following the Pope's life in Poland year by year. He lived as the overwhelming majority of Poles lived. He lived among us, grew up amid Polish joys and sorrows; he was and still remains one of us. It remains to be seen what the rest of his life will bring to him and to us during his Papacy.

Wadowice, a postcard from the beginning of the 20th century

Karol Wojtyła was born on 18 May 1920 in Wadowice, a small town of less than 7,000 inhabitants "at the foot of the Beskid Mały Mountains where the swift current of the River Skawa runs into a broad valley" – according to a local historian. Wadowice, although an old town with a history of over 600 years, has never played a special part in the history of Poland. Property passed from hand to hand by inheritance o purchase. Devastated by epidemics and an amazing number of fires, the town could never have become important although some famous people have been numbered among its inhabitants. One of the most distinguished of them was Marcin Vadovius or Wadowita (1567–1641) who was called after the name of the town. After studying at the Jagiellonian Academy this peasant's son passed through all intermediate posts at the university, finally obtaining the distinction of being made Rector of the Cracow Academy. He provided money for a hospital in Wadowice. Contemporary historians regarded his learning and character very highly and emphasised the fact that he was not only well-known in Poland but abroad also. As early as the 15th century there was a parish school attached to the local church which had been built a century before. In 1772, as a result of the First Partition of Poland among the three powers, Prussia, Russia, and Austria, Wadowice fell under the control of the last-named and the Austrian area was given the German name of *Galizien* (Galicia). In spite of the relatively wide sphere of autonomy which the Poles under Austrian rule possessed (e.g. Polish was the language of the schools and Polish delegates sat in the Austrian parliament), Galicia

The Carpathian Foothills near Wadowice

Above: Mr and Mrs Karol Wojtyła and their son
Karol
Above right: Karol's mother with her other son Edmund

was economically the most deprived area of Poland. The expression
"Galician poverty" dates from this period and was applied first and
foremost to the small towns and villages under Austrian rule. It was
146 years later, in November 1918, that Wadowice was restored to
Poland when the country regained her independence after the
collapse of the Central Powers in the First World War.
The Austrian barracks were taken over by the 12th Infantry
Regiment of the Polish Army. One of the officers in the regiment
was the ensign Karol Wojtyła who worked in the quarter-master's
department. Lt. Wojtyła, his wife Emilia, née Kaczorowska, and
their teenage son Edmund, lived at no. 7, Kościelna Street in
a small upstairs flat in an old tenement building. Wadowice did not
and was not able to change its typical Galician aspect for a long
time. In the market place (today Armii Czerwonej Square) there
were two wells which provided water, for in those days there was no
running water. It was a good job being a "water-carrier" at that
time for such people received payment for fetching water for
households. There was also no drainage system in the town. The
market place was the centre for trade where every Thursday stalls
were set up and market day which was famous throughout the area
took place. Within the town were some small factories – two wafer
biscuit factories, a small steel parts factory, a steam-powered
sawmill, two brickyards, and an artificial fertiliser factory where
bones were treated with sulphuric acid in a very primitive way in the
open air.

10   It is difficult to describe the joy with which the birth of Karol was

Karol Wojtyła, father, with his son Karol

Karol aged 9 (with a ball) among his classmates with Father Stanisław Figlewicz

Altar-boys of Wadowice parish church with Father Figlewicz (Karol seated second from left)

WIELICZKA - 26 V - 1930

greeted in the Wojtyła family. In Volume IV under "C" in the bulky birth register for the years 1917–27 in the local parish church, there is the following entry on page 549: "Natus: 18.V.1920 Carolus Joseph Wojtyła, Roman Catholic, legitimate offspring; parents: Wojtyła, Carolus – father, military official; mother Kaczorowska, Emilia, daughter of Feliks and Maria, née Szolc". And a month later, on 20 June, in the same register: "Wojtyła, Carolus, baptised; godparents: Józef Kućmierczyk, shopkeeper, and Maria Wiadrowska".

Young Karol began to grow up. On fine days his mother, Emilia, took her Loluś (as he was called within the family) to a garden on the other side of the street because their flat did not get the sun and the courtyard was gloomy and dirty. Fourteen year old Edmund was always ready to give her a helping hand.

Karol became bigger and stopped being "little Karol" any more. He ran around, played ball with other children, and did the kinds of things which all children of that age do. At the nursery school run by the Sisters of Nazareth and in the first few years at primary school he was no different from any of the other children, but Mrs Zofia Berchard, who was a teacher at that time at the primary school, noticed that even in the first class he was exceptionally friendly and had rare talents. When he was barely nine years old, his mother died. This was a very heavy loss for Karol who was still a child. After her death he went with his father and brother on a pilgrimage – not for the first time – to the Marian sanctuary at Kalwaria Zebrzydowska. It was always to be the case that at

13

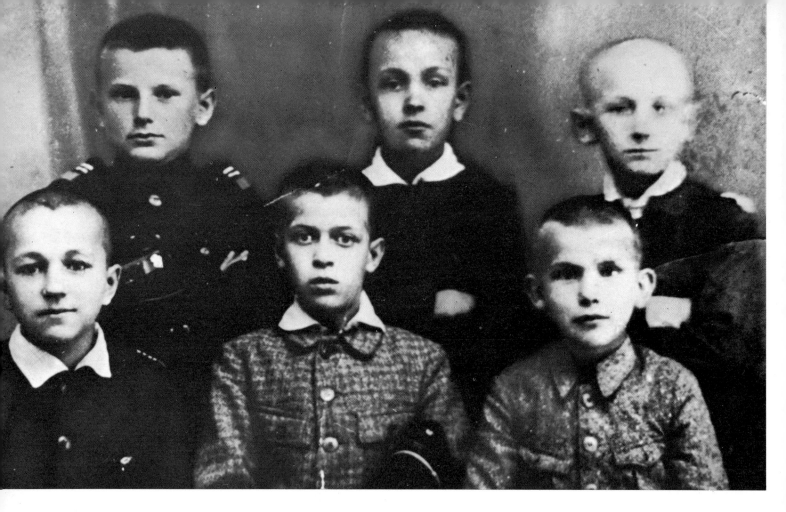

difficult and important times in his life and that of the Church he
would return here.

People in Wadowice still remember the same scenes taking place
day after day after the death of Mrs Wojtyła – father and son going
for a walk, father and son going to and returning from school, father
and son in church. The older son, Edmund, was a medical student in
Cracow at the time and was rarely at home. The father used to do
the washing, the darning, the housework, help Karol with his
homework, and make breakfast and supper. They had dinner across
the street in a well-known local eating house called "Banaś's"
named after the owner. Karol Wojtyła Senior was a man who loved
his son with paternal devotion but was also strict with him. The
home was tidy and orderly and both father and son kept it that way.
It was not a wealthy home; the pension received by Lt. Wojtyła,
who was retired by now, was not a large one, but they muddled
through. The father tried to be a mother for his sons as well as he
was able, although ultimately he did not manage it. Father
Kazimierz Figlewicz who had just arrived in Wadowice at that time
to teach religion at the local high school remembered Karol
Wojtyła, who was in the first year of school, as a boy in whose
behaviour one could perceive the shadow of an early sorrow. Karol
did not only have meetings with the priest at school but also at the
church where he was an altar-boy, and also on the football pitch.
When Father Figlewicz was transferred to Wawel Cathedral in
Cracow after a year's work in Wadowice he did not expect that

Above: **Karol Wojtyła among his
classmates (*top row, first
from left*)**

14 a few years later fate would bring him into such close contact with

Opposite page: **Karol as a school-boy**

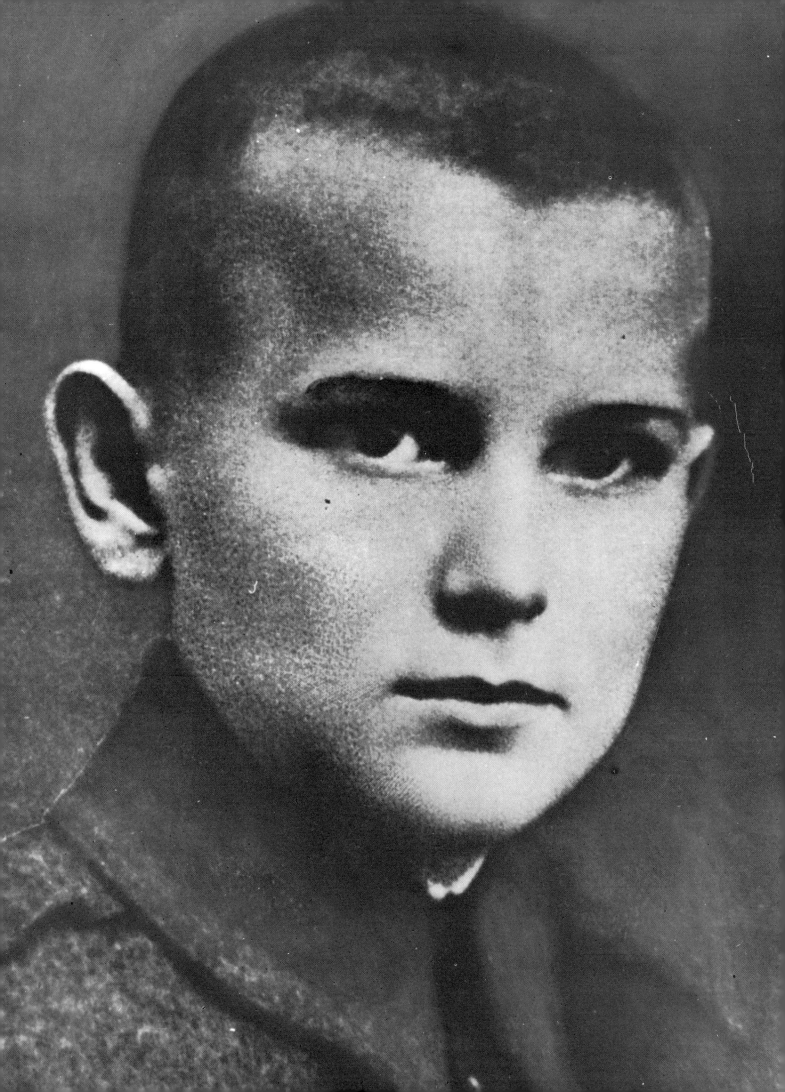

Karol Wojtyła (standing first from left) on the
Wadowice High School outing to Wieliczka in 1936

his former pupil. Father Figlewicz was succeeded by the young
priest Edward Zacher. He also was not to know that in this lively,
talented, clever boy he was to win a friend who would one day be
known to the whole world.

When he was thirteen years of age another bereavement afflicted
the family. Karol's brother Edmund died "as a victim of his
profession in which he had devoted his young life to suffering
humanity", as the inscription on his gravestone reads. Edmund was
barely 27 years old, had just graduated from medical college, and
was a trainee doctor at Bielsko Municipal Hospital. He had
contracted scarlet fever from a patient who in fact recovered and
still today has a requiem mass said every year on the anniversary of
his death at the Franciscan Church in Cracow.

The high school period is one of the most interesting parts of Karol
Wojtyła's life. It was not a time for taking vital decisions for it could
not be and even if he had decided on something he changed his
decisions later in life. However these few years at high school
formed him and paved the way for all his later decisions. It was
a period when he voraciously learned about the world around him.
He discovered the beautiful Beskid Mountains, he read an
enormous variety of books, he acquired a taste for the theatre, he
formed friendships which lasted for years, and most of all he
developed a profound faith. He aroused admiration for the
moderation and equanimity with which he accepted whatever life
brought him. Appearances to the contrary, there was a rich

16 intellectual and cultural life in this provincial town. There was an

Above: The Late Gothic wooden church in Dębno Podhalańskie

Right: Interior of the Dębno church with polychrome work from the beginning of the 16th century

amazing difference between its economic development, which – as has already been mentioned – was practically non-existent, and cultural development. It would in fact be difficult to understand the phenomenon that is Karol Wojtyła and his intellectual development without paying reference to everything which the young high school pupil experienced, which his generation experienced, and without considering the particular atmosphere which prevailed in Wadowice. The homes of the Wadowice intelligentsia even in the Austrian period were first and foremost Polish homes. Here were collections of magnificent historical novels which were read "to cheer the hearts" – *By Fire and Sword, The Deluge* and *The Teutonic Knights* by Henryk Sienkiewicz who was awarded the Nobel Prize in 1905 for his work *Quo Vadis?* Here people gave recitations of poetry by Adam Mickiewicz and Juliusz Słowacki. The home of Karol's closest friend, Zbigniew Siłkowski, was a rehearsal room and concert hall for performances by string quartets and quintets, and there were many other homes like this. Within Wadowice various formal organisations were also active, the aim of which, which was not always so formal, was the maintenance of Polish culture. The Sokół club was active here, an organisation which not only propagated physical fitness with gymnastics and soccer sections but also the spirit of Polish culture. The Municipal Reading Room was an important centre which linked together the various interest groups. People met not only for beer and skittles but also to read Polish books and publications.

18   After independence was regained all of this activity was of course

Above: Wadowice, view of the market place

Above right: The high school in Wadowice attended by Karol Wojtyła. Nearby a monument to the writer Emil Zegadłowicz

Right: Portrait of Marcin Wadowita, the theologian and Rector of Cracow Academy in the 17th century

STANISŁAWA WYSPIAŃSKIEGO

ZYGMUNT AUGUST

Sceny dramatyczne

Obrazy:

1). Ogrody Radziwiłłów
2). Rada królewska
3). Śmierć Barbary
4). Unia Lubelska

Dekoracja witrażowa do sceny II. III. i IV   p. Alina Forysiowa
Ilustracja muzyczna   p. Janina Gärtnerówna
Charakteryzacja   p. Karol Hagenhuber
Inscenizacja i reżyseria   **Mgr Kazimierz Foryś i Karol Wojtyła.**

Orkiestra symfoniczna uczniów Gimnazjum Państw. pod kierow.
prof. **Jana Czubatego.**

Obsada:

Prologos	kol. Zdzisław Przybyło
Augustus	kol. Karol Wojtyła
Barbara	kol. Kazimiera Żakówna
Samuel Maciejowski	kol. Stanisław Małusecki
Jan Tarnowski	kol. Kazimierz Korzeniowski
Jan Sierakowski	kol. Karol Cempiel
Piotr Kmita	kol. Jerzy Peters
Jan Tenczyński	kol. Jan Sarapata
Andrzej Górka	kol. Adam Pukło
Piotr Boratyński	kol. Stanisław Gąska
Lupa Podlodowski	kol. Tadeusz Ponczakiewicz
Rafał Leszczyński	kol. Stanisław Padło
Stanisław Dowojna	kol. Bronisław Byrski
Florian Zebrzydowski	kol. Stanisław Nowak
Herold I.	kol. Włodzimierz Wąchol
Herold II.	kol. Franciszek Haj
Paź I.	kol. Lesław Leśniowski
Paź II.	kol. Franciszek Kassolik

Above: The programme of the school production of *Sigismund Augustus* by Stanisław Wyspiański in 1937

Left: Room in the Wadowice Catechetic Centre where drama productions were performed when Karol was a school-boy

Opposite page: Karol Wojtyła as a student in the Faculty of Arts at the Jagiellonian University in Cracow

The Knight of the Moon by Marian
Niżyński, a production of
the Theatrical Confraternity troupe

intensified. A dramatic society was formed at the Reading Room
and although it was nothing spectacular it is proof of the intellectual
desire to search for something new. A dramatic society was also
founded by the local Church and it had its own auditorium in the
Church Hall and gave performances on socially relevant topics.
Probably the first production was *Judas* by Karol Hubert
Rostworowski, not an easy play even for professionals to act. There
was a third auditorium in the high school which Karol Wojtyła
attended. Mention should also be made of the cultural events in the
nearby town of Gorzeń where there was a regional literary society
called "Czartak" which was particularly active between 1922 and
1929. The founder and prime mover in this group was Emil
Zegadłowicz, the famous writer and poet. Other participants, to
mention just the most famous, were Józef Birkenmajer, Zofia
Kossak-Szczucka, Bolesław Leśmian and Stanisław Ignacy
Witkiewicz. "Czartak" propounded such concepts as the love of
nature, the need for mankind to be reborn through love; it revealed
the inhabitants of the Beskid Mountains as people involved in hard,
everyday toil struggling with the stony, barren mountain soil. The
first copies of their attempts at poetry were published in a printing
house in Wadowice and the high school students learned them by
heart. This poetry described the most basic elements in the lives of
the Beskid population in beautiful language – the hard work, the
search for bread and something better, and the yearning for what
they had lost, the love for the artistic handicrafts of Wowro, a local
self-taught sculptor, especially his birds, his sorrowing Christs and

Actors of the Drama Studio 39 (Karol Wojtyła third from the bottom on the right)

Karol Wojtyła's registration card for his second year of studies (academic year 1939/40)

UNIWERSYTET JAGIELLOŃSKI

Rok akademicki 193*9/40*

KARTA INDYWIDUALNA DLA SŁUCHACZY SZKÓŁ WYŻSZYCH

(Wypełnia k a ż d y student i wolny słuchacz na początku roku akad. Absolwenci, magistranci, doktoranci itp. tej
nie wypełniają).

1. Nazwisko	*Wojtyła*	Imię	*Karol Józef*
2. Nr albumu	*2640*	3. Student czy ~~wolny słuchacz~~	*Student*

I Obecne studia wyższe:		III. Wykształcenie średnie ogólnokształcące:			
1. Wydział (oddział, studium)	*filozoficzny*	Posiada świadectwa	1. dojrzałości	typu	*neoklas.*
				wydane w roku	*1938*
2. Sekcję	*humanistyczną*		2. ukończenia...... klas	typu	
				wydane w roku	
3. Przedmiot główny	*Filolog. polska*		wydane przez szkołę	w miejscowości	*Wadowice*
				w powiecie	*"*
4. Rok studiów (kurs)	*drugi*			w województwie	*Kraków*
				za granicą (kraj)	
II. Poprzednie studia wyższe:		IV. Cechy osobiste kandydata:			

23

Above left: Medieval building of the Collegium Maius of the Jagiellonian University in Cracow

Above: Collegium Novum of the Jagiellonian University, the Rector's Office

The Gothic town hall tower in Cracow Market Place

Wawel Royal Castle in Cracow

his wayside shrines which rose out of his simple soul to adorn rolling landscape. The poems of Zegadłowicz, a pupil of the Wadowice high school, were memorized and not only because they were in the Fourth Year Polish Literature syllabus. All these things were experienced in everyday life and absorbed, unconsciously or not. Before Karol began his first year of high school, his father had to make a choice between the state school and two private schools run by the Pallottine and Carmelite fathers. He chose the state school one assumes for at least three reasons. Firstly because it had a splendid teaching staff and an established reputation (the school had been in existence since 1866 and bore the name of the famous Michał Wadowita); secondly a state school was not as expensive as private schools (we should remember that Lt. Wojtyła as a former state employee was entitled to a 50 per cent reduction in fees); and thirdly (and this is probably the most important reason) schools run by the clergy were of a somewhat different type to state schools, and though they did not take it for granted that each pupil would go on to theological seminary much was being done that many of them followed this path. Mr Wojtyła did not want his son to be subjected to any kind of influence.

In Karol's class there were 32 pupils, the sons of farmers in the area, Wadowice manual workers, and the local professional classes. They formed a close-knit friendly group and in spite of their various social backgrounds they were intellectually on a similar level. Karol was a particular exception in that he could always do everything although none of his fellow pupils were jealous of him for this

27

reason and they never called him a swot. They played soccer with
Karol as goalkeeper and he was a reasonable defender. It
sometimes happened that during a game in the churchyard, playing
around the church walls, they were mercilessly driven away by the
priests. Karol had an incredible memory and knew the whole books
of *Pan Tadeusz* by heart. In his fifth and sixth year of school he read
Kant, Hegel, and Schopenhauer. Zbigniew Siłkowski, who was
called "Lofty" by his pals because he was tall and thin, remembers
that in the presence of Karol he and his colleagues were ashamed of
their ignorance.

It is now difficult to say when Karol first developed his love of the
theatre. A teacher, Mr Bobiński, and his wife infected the boys
with a passion for the theatre and started a theatre group at the
school. They first of all started with play readings, then came
rehearsals, costumes, and emotional satisfaction and success. Then
the Polish teacher Kazimierz Foryś took over the theatre group and
a year later Karol Wojtyła joined the troupe. Even earlier in Polish
classes he had been able to show his best side. As his former teacher
remembers, Karol was extraordinarily gifted in the arts. In literary
analysis of texts he often pointed out details which had escaped the
attention of the teacher and which proved to be important. After
the first few theatre rehearsals it became clear that Karol had great
acting talents, good diction, the ability to "feel" a role, and
naturalness in moving around the stage. He played the leading parts
of Count Henryk in Zygmunt Krasiński's *Undivine Comedy*, Gucio
in Aleksander Fredro's *Maiden Vows*, and Augustus in Stanisław

Above: The 16th century galleries of the Renaissance courtyard in Wawel Castle

Right: The Vasa and Sigismund chapels in Wawel Cathedral

Family grave of the Wojtyłas at Rakowicki
Cemetery in Cracow

30

Mieczysław Kotlarczyk:
założyciel teatru, dyrektor i kierowni

| 1941—1945 |

Karol Wojtyła
Krystyna Dębowska
Halina Królikiewicz
Danuta Michałowska
i inni

1945—1953

Danuta Michałowska
Krystyna Dębowska-Ostaszewska
Halina Królikiewicz-Kwiatkowska
   (—1947)
Janina Bocheńska (1947—)
Jadwiga Bujańska (1951—1953)
Maria Dikówna (1949—1951)

Wyspiański's *Sigismund Augustus*. In the last-named play he was
also stage designer and director of the play with the teacher, Mr
Foryś. Karol understood drama, had splendid ideas, and also was
respected among his colleagues, being able to attract them to
rehearsals. His individuality was not restrained and his youthful
enthusiasm was not restricted which speaks well of his teachers and
the atmosphere which prevailed at Wadowice high school.
He also took part in the dramatic society run by Father Edward
Zacher in the Church Hall. Here the repertoire, although of
a different type to the one at school, was just as ambitious, e.g.
Dante's *Divine Comedy*, not an easy play to be performed even by
professional actors. The last part he was entrusted with by Father
Zacher was that of John the Apostle in Wyspiański's *Apocalypse*
which took place in December 1937 or six months before his school
leaving examination. The whole of Wadowice used to attend these
performances, both in the high school and in the Church Hall.
The drama groups also went to act in Andrychów and Kalwaria
Zebrzydowska nearby. As a reward the young actors were taken to
Cracow to see the legitimate theatre. These were not Karol's first
visits to the city because ever since he had been a small boy he had
gone to visit his aunts there.
In Wadowice he encountered Mieczysław Kotlarczyk, the history
teacher, who had his own vision of the theatre which fascinated
Karol. For hours they sat together in the Kotlarczyk home opposite
Karol's school and in unending discussions dreamt of their vision of
a theatre of words. Sometimes Siłkowski was persuaded to come

31

Left: Zakrzówek Quarry in Cracow

The Solvay chemical plant in Cracow

D.

Należy podawać dokładny adres zamieszkania — zgłaszać bezzwłocznie w kwesturze zmiany adresu. Kto obowiązku tego nie dopełni, naraża się na to, że sprawy dotyczące jego osoby, a w szczególności dyscyplinarne, z powodu niemożności odszukania, będą załatwiane zaocznie.

Rok szkolny 194_5/6_ **Karta wpisowa dla Dziekanatu** Rok studiów: _IV_

Nazwisko:		Imię:		Jest studentem		Wydział
Wojtyła		_Karol_		~~wolnym~~	zwyczajnym	_teologiczny_
Miejsce urodzenia	_Wadowice_	Dzień, miesiąc i rok urodzenia	Religia	Język	Narodowość	Przynależność państwowa	Mieszkanie w Krakowie
							Ul. _Podzamcze_
Powiat	_Wadowice_	_18. V 1920_	_rzym.-kat._	_polski_	_polska_	_Polska_	L. domu: _8_
Województwo	_Kraków_						
Imię i nazwisko rodziców lub opiekuna		_śp. Karol i śp. Emilia_				
Miejsce zamieszkania rodziców lub opiekuna		_nie żyją_				
Stosunek do służby wojskowej		_zwolniony_				
Zakład naukowy, w którym student przebywał w poprzednim roku szkolnym		_Uniw. Jagiell._				

zamierza uczęszczać

Karol Wojtyła's registration card for the Faculty of Theology of the Jagiellonian University for 1945/46

along to the Kotlarczyks by Karol. Out of these meetings in Wadowice came one of the best theatrical companies in Poland – the Teatr Rapsodyczny, founded and headed by Kotlarczyk himself. Karol was first an actor with the company and then a devoted member of the audience.

No one knows whether, when he was at high school, Karol ever thought about becoming a priest. He was an altar-boy and went to church a lot, although he did not make a show of it, something which arose from his own personal needs. For two years he was the chairman of the Sodality of Mary, an organisation which formed part of the Catholic Youth Association. In those days this position was really a great honour for a young boy.

Just before Karol sat for his school leaving examination at the beginning of May 1938 when Archbishop Sapieha of Cracow was about to come on a pastoral visitation to Wadowice, Father Edward Zacher asked Karol to compose and give a speech of welcome. The solemn meeting of the Archbishop and the young people took place in the club room of Wadowice high school where, according to Father Zacher, "Lolek spoke wonderfully well and gave a magnificent speech". During the ceremony the Archbishop noticed the young speaker and was disappointed when he learned from Father Zacher that Karol Wojtyła did not intend to enter a theological seminary. This was their first meeting although it could have been their first and last because Karol had in fact already made his decision, a decision which was regretted not only by Archbishop Sapieha and Father Zacher, but disappointed his

33

fellow pupils too who already knew that he had decided to
study Polish.

On 14 May 1938 Karol passed his school leaving examination with
the top grade. To him fell the honour of making the farewell speech
to the school staff and in the records of the school year 1937/8
written by the headmaster we read the following: "Karol Wojtyła
gave grateful thanks to the teaching staff for all their hard work and
assured them that he and his colleagues would always be guided by
what they had been taught." Then followed the school holidays and
on 1 October he left Wadowice for Cracow to study at the
university. He was to return many times to his home town during
the next few years.

Karol went to live in Dębniki, an old area of Cracow near the River
Vistula, staying with his maternal aunts at no. 10, Tyniecka Street.
Now the city seemed completely different to him from the time
when he used to go there with his family. As an arts student through
and through, he could not have chosen a better place in Poland to
study.

Cracow was and still is an extraordinary city, having a particular
place in the life and history of the Poles. One of the oldest cities in
Poland – the first written references to it date from the 10th century
– according to legend it owes its origin and name to Prince Krak
who slew a dragon and founded a fortified settlement here. Its
subsequent development was due to its favourable geographical
position, on the trade route between Rus, Bohemia, and Western
Europe. In fact Cracow developed very quickly, first as a settlement 35

and later as a town. By 1000 it was already the seat of a bishopric
and it became the capital of Poland in the 11th century. An
increasing number of sacred and secular stone buildings gave the
city fame and importance. Overlooking the city on a limestone hill
loomed the mighty Wawel Castle, the residence of Poland's rulers,
and church spires, first Romanesque and then Gothic, rose over the
city buildings. In one of the churches, the Romanesque Church on
the Rock, a drama took place in 1079 which has been variously
interpreted by historians, a drama which Bishop, Archbishop, and
Cardinal Karol Wojtyła referred to frequently when he lived in
Cracow. A long-standing dispute between Stanislaus of Szczepanów,
Bishop of Cracow, and King Boleslaus the Bold ended in the tragic
death of the former and the excommunication of the latter.
The development of the city was not even halted by the destructive
invasions of the Tartar hordes in the 13th century, for the greatest
period in the history of Cracow was from the 14th to the 16th
centuries. At that time Poland was one of the most powerful states
in Europe and Royal Cracow was the jewel in the Polish crown.
Hither came foreign emissaries and crowned heads. Cracow
Academy, now the Jagiellonian University, the second college of
higher learning to be established in Central Europe after the
University of Prague and before the University of Vienna, was
founded here in 1364 by Casimir the Great, one of the greatest
Polish rulers about whom it is said that he found a Poland of wood
and left a Poland of stone. Cracow merchants carried on their trade
everywhere between Flanders and the Black Sea. Cracow was also

Father Karol Wojtyła, 1946

The parish church of Niegowić near Cracow

a centre for art and the Gothic Cloth Hall was erected here and Wawel royal castle was expanded, as were many churches including the Church of Our Lady, which casts its spell still today, and dozens of houses which were built by the Cracow burghers.

Cracow lost its political importance at the end of the 16th century when the national capital was transferred to Warsaw. In spite of various successive disasters, in spite of numerous foreign invasions, in spite of partitions, Cracow remained an important centre of learning and culture. At the time of the partitions the University of Cracow was one of the two active Polish colleges of higher learning after the closure of the Universities of Warsaw and Vilna by the occupying Russians. At the turn of the 19th and 20th centuries a group of young artists was active in Cracow who called themselves "Young Poland" and whose representatives – painters, writers, and musicians – were the successors of the Romantic movement and constituted a model of art for the whole of Poland. On Floriańska Street in the Jama Michalikowa café there was an artists' cabaret called "The Green Balloon" which was famous all over Poland and brought together the most distinguished writers and journalists, actors and painters in Cracow at that time. It was the conscience of the Cracow population and exercised a great influence on the way people thought in that period. In the 1920's and 1930's the monumental buildings of the Jagiellonian Library, the National Museum, and the Academy of Mining and Metallurgy (the first such institution in Poland) were erected. But first and foremost there was a special atmosphere in Cracow, a city with a centuries-long history

Scenes from the
Cracow countryside

38

and pulsating with youth, a city of avant-garde artists and respectable citizens, a city of dozens of magnificent churches, splendid theatres, museums and winding charming streets. This was the Cracow the eighteen year old Karol Wojtyła arrived at in 1938. He started his studies at the ancient Jagiellonian University which had had the astronomer Nicolaus Copernicus, the writer and politician Andrzej Frycz Modrzewski, and Jan Kochanowski, one of the greatest Polish poets of the Renaissance, among its students. Among the professors who had taught here were such distinguished personalities as Paweł Włodkowic, the lawyer, writer and diplomat, Stanisław of Skalbmierz, the philosopher and expert on theoretical aspects of international law, and Jan Długosz, the historian and diplomat, and author of the first history of Poland. Karol commenced his studies in the Polish department and among his teachers were Kazimierz Nitsch, Stanisław Pigoń, and Kazimierz Wyka, the most famous scholars in this field. Thus one should not be surprised that he committed himself to attending 36 hours of classes a week although according to the university regulations he need only have registered for ten. In spite of this burden of work he still had time for many other activities outside the University. He renewed his old acquaintance with Father Kazimierz Figlewicz, now parish-priest of the Wawel district, to whom he was a regular server at Holy Mass. In his local parish in Dębniki he helped the Salesian Fathers in their work with young people. He was co-editor of the student newspaper *Nasz Wyraz* which the writer and journalist Tadeusz Hołuj recalls in his book *Cyganeria i Polityka:*

39

Countryside near Niegowić

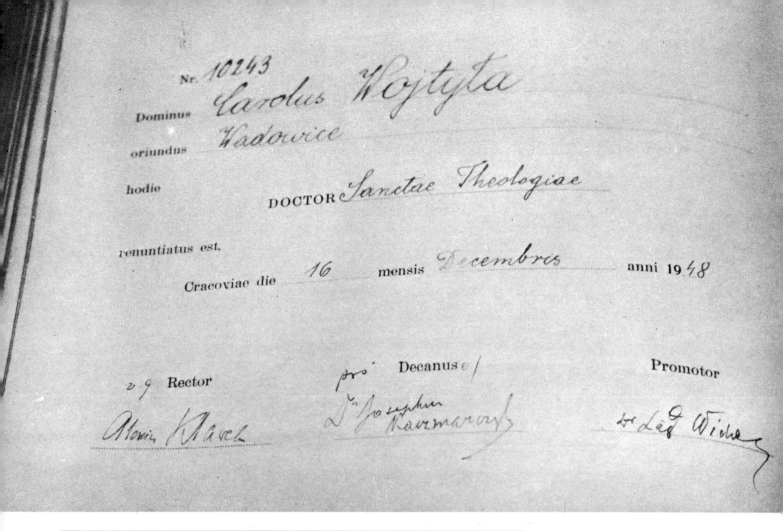

Nr. 10243

Dominus *Carolus Wojtyła*

oriundus *Wadowice*

hodie DOCTOR *Sanctae Theologiae*

renuntiatus est,

Cracoviae die 16 mensis *Decembris* anni 19 48

Rector Decanus Promotor

Page from the Register of the
Jagiellonian University, 1948

St. Florian's Church in Cracow where
Father Wojtyła had his first post in the city

Father Karol Wojtyla, curate

"The newspaper staff used to gather in Karmelicka Street and consisted of students and a few older high school pupils... Zdzisław Nardelli, Wojciech Żukrowski, Tadeusz Kwiatkowski, Juliusz Kydryński, and Karol Wojtyła, a poet." Karol became friends with Juliusz Kydryński and a little later with Tadeusz Kwiatkowski and Wojciech Żukrowski. Kydryński introduced him to many homes in Cracow and presented him as his best friend at the home of the Szkocki and Poźniak families in the Salwator district of the city. These friendships proved to be more than casual acquaintances. Karol and Mrs Szkocka, who he called "Granny", had mutual interests in literature and they talked for hours about Słowacki, Wyspiański, Norwid, and Mickiewicz. At Jadwiga Lewaj's who was friendly with the Szkocki and Poźniak families, Karol learned French.

He was also involved in drama. Tadeusz Kudliński, today a famous writer and theatre expert, had founded a small theatre for young people which was called "The Theatrical Confraternity". This theatre put on a play every May for the noisy celebrations of the Cracow Festival. Karol joined the troupe and made his début in Marian Niżyński's play *Knight of the Moon*. Here he played the part of Taurus, the sign of the zodiac he had been born under and which he did not like. He invited his new-found friends, the Szkockis and the Poźniaks and their families, and other friends, to the first night which was held against the lovely background of the university courtyard of the Collegium Maius. He easily got through his first year at the university and then he had a brief holiday which

was a month shorter that year for on 1 September 1939 the Nazi forces invaded Poland.

Different people have different memories about the first day of the war. Father Figlewicz remembers that the first German air raids on Cracow caused panic among the staff of Wawel Cathedral and he had no one who could assist him at Holy Mass until Karol arrived for confession and Holy Communion. Amid the screaming sirens and the exploding bombs they held the first mass of the war in front of the altar of the Crucified Christ which for the long years of the Occupation became the symbol of Crucified Poland. Within the first few days of September the Germans entered Cracow and selected it as the headquarters of the so-called Government General. The rest of Poland, including Wadowice, was annexed to the German Reich.

The first few weeks of the Occupation in Cracow were not indicative of what was to follow a short time later. Therefore all the greater was the shock when the occupying forces inflicted a stunning blow on the Jagiellonian University. The University Senate had initially thought that the academic year would start, albeit a little later than usual. The students, including Karol, even presented their registration cards at the dean's office. On 6 November a lecture for all professors and academic staff by SS Obersturmbannführer Müller was announced. When the professors had assembled in the Szujski Hall of the Collegium Novum it became clear that as Professor Wyka has said "the lecture was a trap". When the "lecturer" Müller entered the room he was accompanied by German soldiers

Left: The Church of Our Lady in Cracow, one of the most magnificent examples of Gothic ecclesiastical architecture

Below: Altar-piece by Wit Stwosz, a magnificent medieval wood carving in the Church of Our Lady

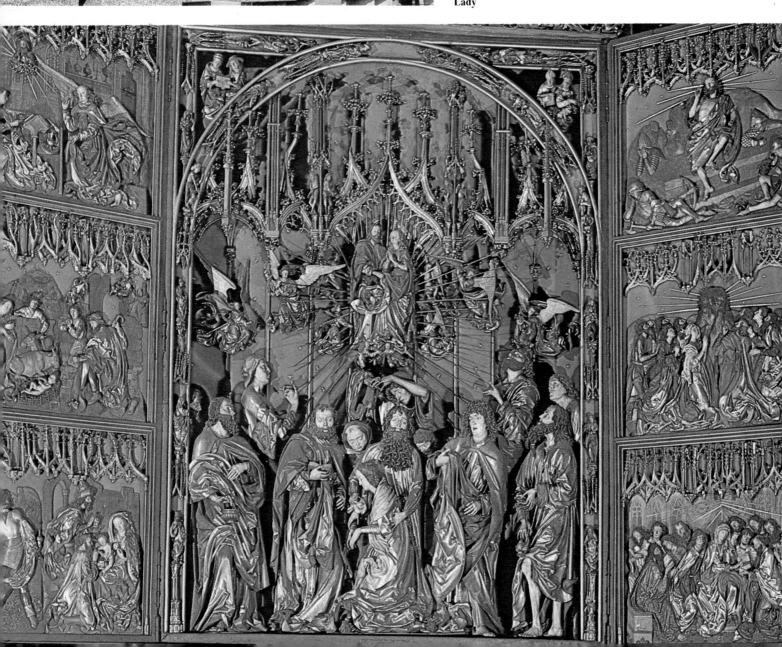

**Interior of the Church of Our Lady during
a solemn service**

Traditional Cracow Christmas crib

47

Father Wojtyła with altar-boys

Opposite page: Kanonicza Street in Cracow

and all the people present, 184 in all, the main body of the University staff, were arrested. This was an unprecedented event, not only in the history of the University of Cracow but in the history of universities in general. The arrest had been skilfully planned and in the records of the notorious Cracow Geheime Staatspolizei it was referred to under the code-name *Sonderaktion Krakau*. All of those who had been arrested were transported deep into the Reich to Sachsenhausen concentration camp. Among them were 18 former or current rectors, 50 deans or sub-deans and 75 ordinary, associate or honorary professors at several Polish or foreign universities, many of them members of international academic institutions.

In Cracow as in the rest of Poland, all secondary schools and colleges of higher learning were shut down. Increased terror, searches, deportations, and shootings did not allow people to have any illusions for the future. The German Institut für Deutsche Ostarbeit, infamous for its criminal activity against Polish learning and culture, arose in place of the Jagiellonian University. Thanks to numerous international diplomatic interventions *Sonderaktion Krakau* did not bring the Germans any advantage, an admission made by the General Governor Hans Frank. In February 1940 they were forced to release some of the Cracow academic staff but 54 of those arrested remained in Sachsenhausen. Among those who did not survive were Professor Stanisław Estreicher, the legal historian and former rector, Professor Jerzy Smoleński, the geographer, Professor Michał Siedlecki, the zoologist, and Ignacy Chrzanowski,

the literary historian. Several other professors died after they returned to Cracow. However, those who were released and had maintained their health and strength resumed their duties in spite of the Nazi terror. At the beginning of 1942 the underground Jagiellonian University started operating with all the departments which it had possessed before the war. Although according to the Nazi regulations anyone who taught or studied would be punished by death, this secret academic instruction lasted for the whole of the Occupation.

Karol Wojtyła both observed and took part in these events. He lived like everyone else, unsure about what the morrow would bring. He had a job and official work entitled him to an *Arbeitskarte* which protected him from round-ups and even permitted him to walk through the city after curfew. At that time there was no concept of "better" or "worse" jobs, for a job *per se* put one in a stronger position by protecting one from deportation for labour in the Reich. Thanks to the influence of his French teacher, Mrs Lewaj, he got a job as a manual worker in the Solvay chemical plant at Borek Fałęcki near Cracow. His fellow students got jobs as waiters, transport guards, shop assistants, caretakers, or even as human hosts for lice breeding in medical research laboratories.

The Solvay works owned some quarries in Zakrzówek near Cracow where the enormous limestone cliffs were blasted by dynamite. The workers broke the rocks up into smaller pieces manually and loaded them on to trucks in which the limestone was transported to the factory

Old-boys reunion at Wadowice High School (Karol Wojtyła second from right)

Opposite page: The Dunajec river gorge in the Pieniny Mountains

Escape from the city

52

His favourite forms of relaxation

Tatra mountains landscape

a few kilometres away. In fact Karol started his work with the
Solvay company at the quarry. He collected together the bits left
over from the quarrying and also went in the trucks for soup for the
workers. His work here brought him into contact with the writer
Wojciech Żukrowski. Everybody who remembers Wojtyła from this
period says that he was taciturn, slim, in fact emaciated, used to
read sitting in corners, and was nicknamed "the student". He always
went about dressed like a worker in wooden clogs and drill
clothes, even on Sundays. On the day before the major Gestapo
raid on the quarry Karol was transferred to the factory which
probably saved his life. He then moved from department to
department, disappearing as suddenly as he had appeared in the
boiler room, the caustic section, the furnace area, the crystallisation
department, etc. He cleaned out pipelines, unfroze pipes, filled
bowls with lye. Once he happened to leave his breviary on the table
in Adam Dyras' office. The two men did not meet again until
several years later when Dyras received an invitation to Father
Wojtyła's consecration as Bishop.

In March 1941 Karol's father, the last of his close relatives, died.
Just after this his old teacher Mr Kotlarczyk and his wife moved in
with Karol and once again for many hours they talked about the
theatre and revived their plans to create a theatre of words as they
had done back in Wadowice. They founded a theatre without sets,
costumes, lights or props, something which not only arose from
artistic concepts but also from security considerations. This theatre
was founded in fact at a time when all the theatres in Cracow were

nur für Deutsche ("only for Germans"), when it was forbidden to listen to the radio, when no literary or cultural magazines existed at all. It was of course an underground theatre. Rehearsals and performances took place in various friendly Cracow homes – at the Kydryńskis, the Kwiatkowskis, at Karol's, and at the Poźniaks. It was at the home of the last-named family that the first performance of *Samuel Zborowski* by Juliusz Słowacki was given. The audience consisted of about 20 people and the atmosphere was sophisticated and exciting. During the whole Occupation period this troupe staged 22 productions including seven first performances. The moving spirit of the group was the incomparable director Mieczysław Kotlarczyk while Karol as an actor was much praised by the audiences. Drama was an escape, an escape from reality, an act of self-preservation. In this respect it was similar to studying at the underground Jagiellonian University. That was also a kind of self-preservation, something which preserved and protected people from breaking down and even introduced them to the idea of learning something new for its own sake as it was not clear what value this learning would be. Nearly 1000 students were involved in secret classes. Karol started studying at the beginning of 1942 but he did not resume the studies which he had started before the war but began studying theology.

In his choice of this path in life the personality of Jan Tyranowski, a modest tailor from Dębniki, played a large part. They met at the home of the Salesian Fathers in the Dębniki parish which was under

the invocation of St. Stanisław Kostka. The Salesians were concerned

He loved to return to the mountains

with the education of young men as the regulations of their order commanded them. Today, following the Second Vatican Council this work is called the Apostolate of the Laity. Tyranowski had had a mystical bent since birth and was a kind of Catholic guru; he was also amazingly well-read and had an impressive knowledge of Christian literature. He led a group to which Karol belonged and the latter regarded him as his spiritual leader. They read the Bible, the works of St. John of the Cross, and various other writings together. Constant improvement of self and striving to reach God was Tyranowski's creed. Some years later Father Wojtyła wrote an article in the Cracow weekly *Tygodnik Powszechny* entitled "An Apostle" and said about Tyranowski: "He was an apostle of divine greatness, of divine beauty, and divine transcendentalism. He learned this from his chief spiritual guide, St. John of the Cross." Wartime classes consisted of lectures held each time in a different place all over Cracow. They involved working by day, studying at night under threat of constant fear and sometimes death. "The Faculty of Theology was one of the most severely hit departments during the war," said theology professor Tadeusz Glemma, who had been dean of the underground Faculty of Theology during the war, during the inauguration of the first academic year after the war, "because it lost more than half of its professors and lecturers and predominantly those who could have worked for many years longer for the good of Polish learning." Karol Wojtyła escaped round-ups, searches, and deportations. Even during the so-called "Black Sunday" which the Germans imposed on the inhabitants of Cracow

Interior of the Catholic University of Lublin

in retaliation for the Warsaw uprising which had just started, on the first Sunday in August 1944, nothing happened to him. "Black Sunday" was an example of pacification on a grand scale. Anybody caught on the streets was deported; people were dragged from their homes and taken to police patrol wagons, and those who tried to escape were shot. The Germans hauled in everybody living in the nearby houses on Tyniecka Street and even in the house where Karol was living but they did not come to get Karol at all even though his apartment was not locked. Many of those taken away never returned. On the following day the Archbishop of Cracow, Adam Sapieha, summoned all the theology students to the Bishops' Palace and hid them there until the end of the war. Karol did not return to the Solvay factory. The German officials of the factory searched with great thoroughness for the fugitive but he did not emerge from the Bishops' Palace until liberation. Of course only the name remained of the prewar palace. The students slept on three-tiered bunks and the food was very meagre even though the Archbishop shared everything he had with his lodgers. Archbishop Sapieha, social reformer, organiser, benefactor, and ardent patriot, had great influence among the entire community. Right during the first days of September 1939 he assumed the leadership of the Citizens' Aid Committee. The Committee dispensed material assistance to the families of officers and soldiers who had been killed or captured by the enemy. The Archbishop was also one of the co-organisers of underground classes at the Jagiellonian University. In addition, he supported and protected the armed resistance

STRON 8   POLEMIKA NA TEMAT IBL (K. WYKA, M. DŁUSKA)   CENA Zł 3.50

TYGODNIK POWSZECHNY

JAK TO JEST Z TYM "ŚWIATOPOGLĄDEM NAUKOWYM"?

Ks. KAROL WOJTYŁA

ELEMENTARZ ETYCZNY (7)

MORALNOŚĆ A ETYKA

Ks. KAROL WOJTYŁA

ELEMENTARZ ETYCZNY

PROBLEM ETYKI NAUKOWEJ

KAROL WOJTYŁA

ELEMENTARZ ETYCZNY (8)

HUMANIZM A CEL CZŁOWIEKA

KATOLICKI
ZAKŁAD WYCHOWAWCZY
pod Warszawą
poszukuje wychowawców w wieku
od 19 do 30 lat. Wykształcenie od
małej matury wzwyż. Podania pro-
simy przesyłać do redakcji
"Tygodnika Powszechnego".

Two of Karol Wojtyła's many publications

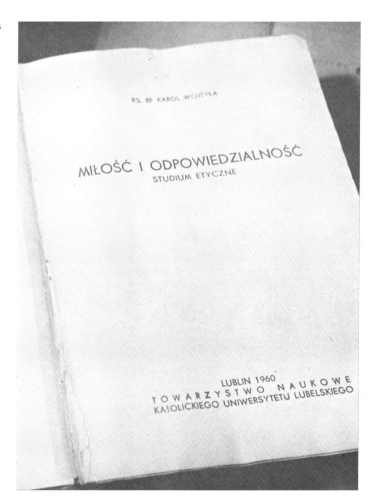

movement and placed many priests as chaplains at the disposal of the Home Army.

In gratitude to his great predecessor Cardinal Wojtyła had money raised for a monument opposite the Bishops' Palace at the Franciscan Church in Cracow.

Freedom, although long expected, came suddenly to Cracow on 17 January 1945. The Nazis had made preparations for blowing up the city and had placed mines everywhere, including the most splendid buildings in the city, but they did not succeed in carrying out their work of destruction and had to make a hasty withdrawal from the city. The Soviet divisions of General Konev, warned of the danger, had surrounded the city. This outflanking manoeuvre saved the priceless historical buildings, thanks to which Cracow is today listed among the most splendid cities of its kind in the world.

Poland had emerged triumphant from the war with Germany but had suffered losses which per head of population were among the greatest for the countries which took part in the war. Over six million Polish citizens had died in concentration camps or on the various fronts and 38 per cent of the prewar national wealth had been destroyed.

Cracow was free. The University emerged from the underground and when the new academic year was inaugurated in March, Karol was in his fourth year of theological studies. Normal life began again. In accordance with the regulations Karol rarely left the theological seminary but Mr Kotlarczyk, who was at that time engaged in organizing the Teatr Rapsodyczny, came to see him.

After all these years Zbigniew Siłkowski was able to come over from Wadowice and others who came to see him were Mrs Szkocka, Mrs Poźniak, Aunt Maria Wiadrowska and his Kaczorowski aunts, and of course Tyranowski.

In August 1946 Karol took his final examinations in theology. Of the 26 examinations which he had to sit in his final semester, he achieved the highest possible marks in 19, the next highest in 6, and the third highest in only one (psychology). On 1 November 1946, in the private chapel of Cardinal Sapieha, Karol Wojtyła was ordained as a priest. All of his Cracow and Wadowice friends were present for the ceremony. One of the three masses which he celebrated on that day in Wawel Cathedral was dedicated to his three closest deceased relatives – his mother, father, and brother. On the following day he said mass in his own parish in Dębniki with the Salesians after which there was a celebration with those closest to him at the Poźniaks. In actual fact this was Father Wojtyła's farewell before departing for studies abroad. On the first Sunday of November he performed a celebration of Holy Mass at the parish church in Wadowice. His old school scripture teacher Father Edward Zacher preached a beautiful sermon and was not to know at the time that in the future he would give another four sermons in connection with the life of Karol Wojtyła. In the thick register of births, under the name of his former pupil, he wrote: "Ad ordinem presbiteratus 1.XI.1946" ("ordained 1.XI.1946").

There was another gathering at the Siłkowski home and people recalled their school days and those who had been taken away by

In Zakopane with Father Józef Gąsiorowski

Pamiętaj, że przez

Sakrament Bierzmowania

którego Ci dzisiaj udzieliłem,
zobowiązałeś się odważnie wyznawać

Wiarę Świętą

i według Niej postępować.

Na tę drogę życia
prawdziwie chrześcijańskiego
błogosławię Ci z całego serca

+ Karol Wojtyła
arcybiskup
metropolita krakowski

Kraków, dn. 12. 4. 1964.

Interior of the Bishops' Palace in Cracow

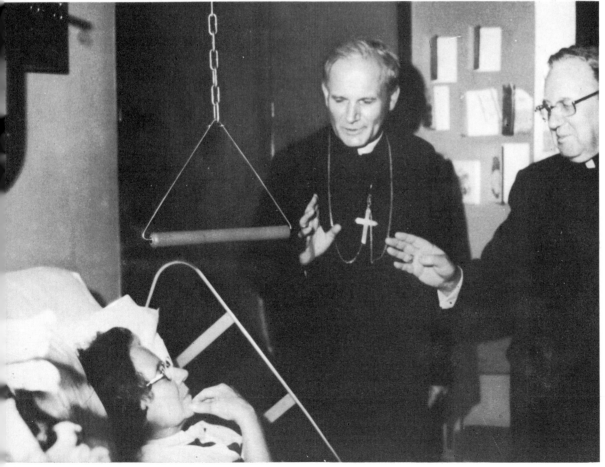

Pastoral duties of the Archbishop of Cracow

the war. Then Father Wojtyła set off on his first journey to Rome –
he was to return to Poland two years later.

Karol arrived in Rome in the middle of November. He was to work
on his doctorate in philosophy at the famous Pontifical Angelicum
University run by the Dominicans. The subject of his doctoral
dissertation was to be the doctrine of St. John of the Cross. He had
decided on this subject long before, when Jan Tyranowski had
introduced him to the work of this 16th century Spanish Discalced
Carmelite. St. John of the Cross had fascinated Karol so much that
even when he was studying at the underground seminary and also
for a long time later, when he was a priest, he always wondered
whether he should not join the Discalced Carmelite Order.

In Rome he lived at the Collegio Belga on the Via del Quirinale.
His studies in Rome involved an enormous amount of work but he
managed to cope with it splendidly. He was fascinated by the
Reverend Professor Reginald Carrigou-Lagrange who supervised his
work and planned his course of studies. In a letter to Zofia Poźniak
of 27 March 1947 he wrote, "I think that a lot could be said about
Thomist studies... this entire system is not only something extremely
clever but, at the same time, something extremely beautiful and
inspiring, and on top of that, simple. It seems to me that profound
thoughts do not require many words. The more profound they are,
the more superfluous words become." He delved into the writings of
St. John of the Cross and he learned Spanish to be able to read the
works in the original. No translations, not even the best ones, can

render the essence of something as delicate as a philosophical text,

77

Karol told his students and Ph.D. candidates later when urging them to learn foreign languages. In 1978, during his last visit as Cardinal to the Federal Republic of Germany, three months before the Conclave, he explained to his hosts who complained of the lack of German translations of Polish philosophical works that if they wished to learn about Polish philosophical thought, they should study it in Polish.

Karol's studies in Rome also introduced him to an hitherto unknown magnificent city. In the same letter to Zofia Poźniak he wrote, "Another wonderful experience has been venturing into Rome, an experience which cannot be described in few sentences. It has so many aspects and levels, so many details which make one richer, but still far away from a general approach to these experiences. Deo gratias! God willing, we shall talk about all of this together someday..." While in Rome he missed his friends in Cracow and wrote, "Please give my very best wishes to everybody at Lipki [the Szkocki household – T. K.], to the Włodzimierz family in Dębniki, to Piotr and Marysia, to Jadwiga, the Kułakowskis, Mrs. Burowa, and all other friends." He remembered everybody and wrote to them with differing degrees of frequency, not forgetting namedays, birthdays, and anniversaries. He would always be as considerate regardless of the amount of work and number of duties. He also waited for letters of which there were never enough but which were necessary for him and which he missed a lot. He knew of the incurable illness afflicting Tyranowski who was in hospital and was unable to write although he was constantly asking about his

Opposite page: **The Baroque sarcophagus of St. Stanislaus in Wawel Cathedral**

79

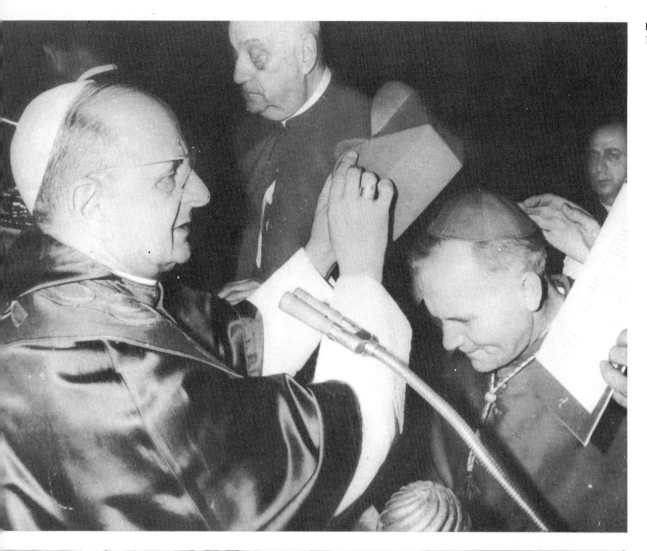

Karol Cardinal Wojtyła, 1967

Polish bishops during an audience with Pope Paul VI

The ceremonial handing over of the stone from the grave of St. Peter to Cardinal Wojtyła and Father Józef Gorzelany by Pope Paul VI

former disciple. "Many thanks to Granny [Irena Szkocka – T. K.] for all the important news about Jan. In reply I enclose a letter for our beloved Job. Time and time again this is how things happen. This is how the Lord destroys those who have willingly sacrificed themselves to Him for such destruction..." Jan Tyranowski never read the letter for he had died of tuberculosis a week before it arrived.

Karol's first year of studies was drawing to an end. Once again let us read an extract from a letter dated July 1947: "The last few weeks of the academic year were a period of strenuous work before the licentiate examination, i.e. an examination on the whole of Christian theology. Thanks God the exam is now over and I can think more clearly. For a change I am now writing from Paris which I have managed to get to, stopping at Marseilles and Lourdes on the way. It's been the Prince's [Cardinal Sapieha – T.K.] wish that I should visit France, Belgium and maybe Holland during this holiday, and learn the methods of pastoral work in these countries. This is an immeasurable job and what is achieved depends on the Grace of God and one's own perception of its workings. I'm not only looking at the work of priests but also the historic Gothic monuments which can be seen here, in Northern France and Flanders..."

While learning about methods of pastoral work he was also active in the Young Christian Workers movement (*Jeunesse Ouvrière Chrétienne*) and ministered to Polish communities there. "Believe me," he wrote from Rome on 25 February 1948, "time is rushing by at an amazing speed. I don't really know how the last 18 months *81*

have sped by. My studies, observations, and meditation have all
spurred me on so that each day has been completely filled. This also
makes me feel that I am serving God according to my capabilities
and according to His Will by which my superiors have appointed
me. Thus the most important thing is not only not to squander
a rare personal opportunity. I have constantly kept my spiritual link
with Poland in my thoughts, my prayers, and my reading." He
returned to Poland in June 1948 and although later he was to travel
all over the world this journey to Rome was to remain for Father
Wojtyła the most fruitful and the most interesting of his journeys, if
also the most difficult because it lasted the longest length of time,
and he did not like to stay away from Poland for too long.
Immediately after his return to Poland Cardinal Sapieha dispatched
Father Wojtyła to his first job in a parish in Niegowić, a God-
forsaken hamlet near Cracow. He arrived in Niegowić on 18 July
1948, as can be read in the Register of Priests of that parish. He
came on foot from Gdów and years later Stanisław Substelny was to
recall his first meeting with Father Wojtyła: "He was walking from
Gdów. He wore shabby trousers, a waistcoat, worn-out shoes, and
carried a briefcase that I would be ashamed to take with me to
market. He asked me the quickest way to get to Niegowić. I asked
him why he wanted to go there and he answered that he was
going to work in the parish. He went away and knelt before
a wayside shrine which still stands there today. He prayed for
a long time and then he got up and went the way I told him."

82 He was barely 13 months in Niegowić but he accomplished a lot. He

*Opposite page: The Cathedral in Gniezno
where the first Polish archbishopric was
established in 1000*

St. Adalbert's sarcophagus in Gniezno Cathedral

The door of Gniezno Cathedral (detail), one of the most splendid Romanesque works of art in Poland, showing the life and death of St. Adalbert

often went across the River Raba to visit the poorest people on the
other side of the river. Tadeusz Turakiewicz remembers that "There
was a woman from Klęczany who was called Tadeuszka. She once
came to see Father Wojtyła to complain to him that she had been
robbed. He gave her what he had, even a pillow and eiderdown." It
even made people a bit angry for they had just bought him
everything because he had slept on bare boards. He was often seen
at prayer even when taking an early morning walk in the direction
of Wiatowice, or walking around the church, or sitting alone in one
of the pews. People liked his sermons very much. He celebrated
masses, performed baptisms and marriages, and conducted religious
instruction; he did everything a curate should do. At the same time
he completed the academic work he had started in Rome and
prepared himself for his examination at the Jagiellonian University.
Therefore he often went to Cracow, mainly by bicycle, 40
kilometres each way. During one of these bicycle rides, he stopped
at the rectory in Wieliczka where he met the young curate, Józef
Gorzelany. Neither of them knew at that time, though they
immediately took to each other, that one day they would together
build one of the most splendid churches in Poland, in Nowa Huta, the
working class district of Cracow, which did not exist at that time.
On 24 November 1948 Father Wojtyła took his final M.D. oral
examination at the Faculty of Theology of the Jagiellonian
University and less than a month later passed, on 16 December, his
final D.D. oral examination on his dissertation (which had been
written in Latin) concerning the doctrine of St. John of the Cross.

This did not mean he was no longer concerned with Jan
Tyranowski, for many years later, when Cardinal, he urged Father
Kacz to write a study of this unusual man.

It is worth mentioning Niegowić again for one other reason. We find
in the Parish Register that "when our pastor, Monsignor Buzała,
celebrated the 50 years of his ministry on 15 May 1949, Father
Wojtyła organised a meeting of parishioners in the Church Hall.
There was much discussion about the best way of celebrating the
jubilee. Some people wanted to buy something, some wanted to
paint the fence round the Church, and others wanted to tidy up the
village, but Father Wojtyła said that the best present for the
Monsignor would be to celebrate this anniversary by building a new
church." And that is exactly what happened. On 17 August 1949
Father Wojtyła returned to Cracow, having been transferred to the
parish of St. Florian. His former parishioners in Niegowić completed
the building of a new church, the first church to be built at the
instigation of Karol Wojtyła.

His two year period of work at the parish of St. Florian was the next
stage of Karol Wojtyła's links with Cracow. In fact it was exactly at
this time and in this place that he revealed his exceptional talent for
working with young people. His contacts with his congregation did
not end in the church. He spent his leisure with them, went to the
cinema, theatre, and concerts with them, made trips outside
Cracow, mainly by bike, with them, and spent his free days and
holidays with them. Young people were drawn to him and he felt
86 easy among them. He also had contact with them through the

Catholic Youth Association. He lectured to them and chatted with them, often during trips outside Cracow too.

At St. Florian's he also met adults, often quite famous academics. At a meeting with such a group of people a famous expert on the history of philosophy Professor Stefan Swieżawski once gave a paper on the late Middle Ages. During the course of the discussion which took place after the lecture, the professor noticed the young priest and his clear perception, his lively and profound reactions, and his knowledge. From that time on their meetings became more and more frequent and usually took place in the home of the professor on Krupnicza Street where in the persons of Mrs Maria Swieżawska, the professor's wife, and their daughters, Maja and Heluś, Father Wojtyła discovered more friends. And once again it was a friendship which lasted for years. He also continued to visit the Szkocki, Poźniak, and Kotlarczyk families. Karol used to go to visit his friends or the Teatr Rapsodyczny either by himself or in the company of other priests. His period as assistant at St. Florian's, although fruitful from the point of view of his pastoral work, did not allow Father Wojtyła enough time to pursue his studies. In the middle of 1951 Archbishop of Cracow Cardinal Adam Sapieha relieved him of this post and granted him a sabbatical during which he was to work on post-doctoral research.

Cardinal Sapieha died on 23 July 1951. His death took place at a time when his help would have been invaluable for the young priest in his pastoral work. The future Polish Pope had to carry on his work and develop in conditions which were by no means easy.

Celebrations of 1000 years
of Christianity
in Poland in Cracow

90

On 1 September 1951 Father Wojtyła moved into no. 21,
Kanonicza Street, a twisting street lined with small terraced
medieval houses, beneath Wawel hill. He loved this house and the
quiet street whence he was later to escape even from the Bishops'
Palace. As subject for his post-doctoral research he chose the
phenomenological ethics of the German philosopher Max Scheler
who lived at the turn of the 19th century. Scheler's doctrine was
close to the beliefs of Wojtyła, in that the former first and foremost
dealt with a practical philosophy. According to Father Wojtyła
philosophy should not be only a pure academic subject but a tool
intended for helping other people. In the second half of 1953 he
took his oral examination for his post-doctoral degree at the Faculty
of Theology at the Jagiellonian University on the subject of his
thesis, i.e. "An Evaluation of the Implications of Max Scheler's
Philosophy for a Model of Christian Ethics". One of his reviewers
was Professor Swieżawski and Father Wojtyła's work on his thesis
linked the two men even closer together in spite of their different
opinions as to conceptual solutions. The examination went off well
although as far as Professor Swieżawski was concerned the question
as to whether Scheler's philosophy could serve as a method for
interpreting Christian ethics was a controversial one. Karol Wojtyła
was awarded the rank of assistant professor by a decree of the
Central Academic Qualifications Commission on 31 October 1957.
His dissertation was published by the Academic Association of the
Catholic University of Lublin in 1959.
This dissertation marked out an academic career for Father

Wojtyła. On 1 October 1953 he was appointed Professor of Moral
Theology and Social Ethics at Cracow Seminary. He gave lectures
there on social ethics which were attended by the young priest
Tadeusz Styczeń who later became one of Professor Wojtyła's
closest collaborators.

Cooperation between Professor Wojtyła and the Catholic University
of Lublin started in 1954. Professor Swieżawski, who had worked at
the Lublin College since 1946, decided to win Karol over for the
Catholic University. A centre for philosophy had in fact been
formed in Lublin for which the relatively young Catholic University,
the only university of its kind in Poland or this part of Europe, was
soon to become famous. The University was founded in 1918 by
Father Idzi Radziszewski with money donated by Karol Jaroszyński
and with the support of Marian Fulman, Bishop of Lublin, and the
broad masses of the Polish Catholic community. The aim of the
University was and continues to be to educate a Catholic intellectual
élite. The University was established in former monastery buildings
in which, after a general renovation, four faculties were housed –
Theology, Canon Law, Law and Social Sciences, and Arts. The slow
but systematic development of the University ceased in 1939. The
Nazis turned the building into a barracks and a German military
hospital, and destroyed academic equipment, room fittings, and the
library collections. They arrested many professors and students,
some of whom perished. After the war in September 1944 the
Catholic University recommenced classes in all faculties, as the first

92 university to do so. In 1946 the Faculty of Philosophy was created,

which gathered together some splendid academics, as well as
Departments of History of Art and English. In the 1950's,
Professor Swieżawski offered Father Wojtyła a post in Lublin.
In the academic year 1954/55 Father Wojtyła held
the post of Lecturer in Ethics in the Faculty of Christian
Philosophy at the Catholic University.
It was both an extremely difficult and, paradoxically enough,
extremely favourable period for the Faculty. "External
circumstances could not have been more severe," says Professor
Swieżawski today, but in spite of this the Faculty developed, albeit
slowly. A group of highly qualified academics, representing various
philosophical disciplines, was assembled here. They created
a Philosophy Department at the University which came to be known
as the Lublin School, both at home and abroad. The moving spirit of
the group was Jerzy Kalinowski, ex-officio Dean of the Faculty and
an expert in logic and legal philosophy. The staff also included the
Dominican metaphysician Father Mieczysław A. Krąpiec, the experts
in the history of philosophy, Stefan Swieżawski, and Marian
Kurdziałek, the methodologist Father Stanisław Kamiński and the
ethics teacher Karol Wojtyła. Usually they gathered at Professor
Kalinowski's home and conducted long philosophical discussions. All
in all they were people of different backgrounds with a similar
orientation. They found common agreement in the philosophy of
St. Thomas Aquinas although each of them interpreted his relevance
for modern times in a different way. Father Wojtyła perhaps most of
all wanted to apply 13th century Thomism to contemporary times.

These discussions gave rise to various writings which became known
both in Poland and abroad, which in turn made the Catholic
University an important centre for philosophical thought in Poland.
Every two weeks Father Wojtyła used to go from Cracow to Lublin
for two or three days of classes, trips which involved the whole night
on the train, a whole day of lectures and seminars, and late in the
evening meetings with the other teaching staff. Sometimes he was so
tired that, for example, during seminars on metaphysics it was with
difficulty that he controlled his fatigue and drowsiness, as Professor
Antoni Stępień, the famous phenomenologist, remembers today.
He used to travel from Cracow with other lecturers, sometimes with
Father Franciszek Tokarz, sometimes with Professor Swieżawski.
Father Wojtyła was an ever more frequent guest at the Swieżawski
family home in Krupnicza Street. He was the spiritual guardian of
their children and there was no family anniversary at which he was
not present. Professor Swieżawski had a visitors' book which all his
guests signed, Karol Wojtyła included. The entry for Christmas Day
says "Carols" followed by several signatures including Karol
Wojtyła's. Young and old sat there till late at night singing carols.
In 1956 Father Wojtyła became head of the Department of Ethics
at the Catholic University and he has continued in this post without
a break until the present time. In spite of other, possibly more
responsible, duties he has remained loyal to the University and
above all to ethics. This was a period when he was very much
involved in the work of the Lublin school of philosophy. He began
to gather around him a group of young people for whom he was

95

The coronation of the Image in
Smardzewice, Kielce diocese

something more than just a university teacher. One of the largest
halls at the University was always overcrowded for his lectures and
the young people sat in the benches, on the benches, on the
window-sills, and on the floor. Like previously at St. Florian's in
Cracow so now too he did not give dry theoretical talks in spite of
the vast quantity of knowledge he had. His idea of ethics was rooted
in everyday life. He taught the students that to be an ethics scholar
was not only a question of intellect, acquaintance with various
theories, or the possession of more or less general knowledge. To be
an ethics scholar it was necessary to maintain harmony between
knowledge and everyday behaviour. For him ethics did not mean art
for art's sake. Moral problems which life brought gave rise to the
necessity for deep reflection and productiveness in this field. The
product of this reflection should be of service in practical activities.
But practice meant a man conditioned in various ways, not
preconditioned but postconditioned, it meant people and relations
between people among whom the most important thing was love.
He talked wonderfully about love and this was his favourite subject.
The students listened to him and watched him intently; they saw the
threadbare sleeves of his cassock, his worn-out shoes, and always
the same greenish, shabby coat, worn with a turned-up collar.
However few students knew that Father Wojtyła earmarked half of
his university salary (and all of his salary when he became a bishop)
to help needy students. Even those who benefited from this help did
not know where it came from. They did not get it for nothing,
however, but did work in the Ethics, Metaphysics, and History of

96

Opposite page: **Karol Cardinal Wojtyła
with Pope Paul VI**

Academic staff of the Catholic University of Lublin

Philosophy Departments, lent books, issued library cards, etc. As a result they thought that their money came from the University pay department; only a few, those who were near to him, were in on the secret. He was very often seen praying – in the breaks between lectures, in the lecture halls or corridors he would step aside to pray. He did not do it ostentatiously and people felt that it was genuine. Outside the lectures he did not say much and was not the kind of person who immediately got on close terms with everyone. He preferred to listen attentively and looked searchingly at the speaker. However, when anyone needed help they knew that they could always count on him. That is probably why in fact people were attracted to him and trusted in him. They confided their problem to him, not only academic ones but religious and moral ones too. In asking questions he extracted the truth from the person he was speaking to to enable him to come to a decision. The students did not mind that he was always turning up late. To the customary "academic 15 minutes" he would always add another 15 minutes, thus starting his classes at half past the hour, and he would apologise by saying, "You know that my life is governed by Cracow time". It remained a mystery how it happened that a man who was so disciplined within himself always came late.

In the course of his lectures, seminars and examinations at Lublin – during which, incidentally, he was not too demanding, a fact which made his students doubly ashamed when they could not cope with the subject – he chose a team of those closest to him, those interested in ethics. His favourite "children" were Sister Miriam

The reading room at the Catholic University of Lublin

Szymeczko and Father Tadeusz Styczeń, and later, Sister Karolina Kasperkiewicz, Sister Józefa Zdybicka, Jerzy Gałkowski, Stanisław Grygiel, and Jan Bardan. A new idea which he introduced into the Ethics Department was the holding of seminars outside, among the forests, hills, lakes, and rivers. Also the first all-university meetings, called "The Philosophical Weeks", took place on the Mazurian Lakes. During one of these weeks, when every day ended with a bonfire, games for everyone and songs, the young people called Father Wojtyła "Uncle". The name stuck not only for the students in Lublin but for all people all over Poland who were a bit younger and so near to him.

Several years' work at the Catholic University of Lublin resulted in many articles which Father Wojtyła had published in such journals as *Collectanea Theologica, Ateneum Kapłańskie, Znak, Polonia Sacra, Roczniki Filozoficzne KUL*, and *Tygodnik Powszechny*, in which he wrote about St. John of the Cross and the ethics of Max Scheler. These included both extracts of articles written earlier and new ideas on the subject. In 1957 and 1958 he wrote a series of 21 articles in *Tygodnik Powszechny* under a headline "Ethics for Beginners". This series contained the basic principles of ethics which no one had ever explained to Polish Catholics hitherto. In one of these articles (*Tygodnik Powszechny*, no. 1, 1958), Karol Wojtyła wrote: "Christian ethics not only protects the very social virtues which are such a priceless legacy of the Revelation of Christ, but also protects the very foundations of these virtues in man and their raison d'etre in the individual human being. A person is a free

The Reverend Professor Karol Wojtyła with the
Reverend Dr Tadeusz Styczeń, and (*below*) the
Reverend Professor Mieczysław A. Krąpiec,
Rector of the Catholic University of Lublin

During Ecclesiological Week at the
Catholic University of Lublin

Ceremony of awarding a doctorate
to Jerzy Gałkowski

Above right: Professor Karol Wojtyła with
Dozent Teresa Rylska

In the courtyard of the Catholic University
of Lublin

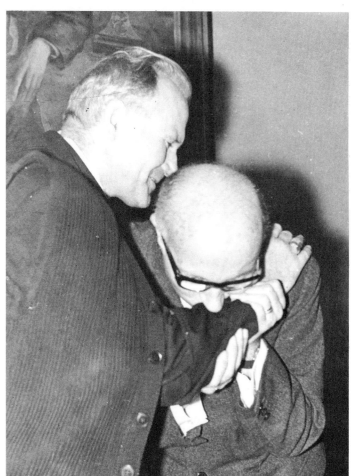

With Professor Stefan
Swieżawski

A medal for Pope John Paul II on the
occasion of the 60th anniversary of the
Catholic University of Lublin

being but this freedom does not mean a detachment from society, a person is a free being within the framework of social life. He makes good use of his freedom when he develops real social virtues on the natural basis of his inclination to social life. These virtues at the same time determine the fulfilment of the common good. A human being cannot develop and improve without this common good." Under the pen-name of Andrzej Jawień he published poetry. Echoes of his job at Zakrzówek during the Occupation can be found in his poem *The Quarry:*

> Listen to the steady beats of the hammers
> Which are carried into the breasts of men
> To test the strength of the blows.
> Listen – the current cleaves the pebbly river with its power
>
> And a thought arises within my mind,
> A thought that comes day after day,
> That the real greatness of this work
> Is found in the hearts of men.

Contemporary unease was the subject of a beautiful and profound poem entitled *Profiles of a Cyrenaic:*

> Don't mention a name. Link any "I" with
> Everything which opens and closes before drawing breath,
> Everything which sometimes dies in the climate of the heart,
> Which haunts man for whole days
> Which changes light into night and warmth into cold...

He did not wish anything "to die in the climate of the heart" but
above all he did not wish man "to die in the climate of the heart".
Out of this uneasiness came one of Father Wojtyła's best works on
ethics, *Love and Responsibility*. In this book the author tries to
show what genuine love depends on and what responsibility for
oneself and for other people means. According to the basic thesis of
this work, the threat to personal dignity is not effected exclusively
by external factors and events. Man is most threatened by the fact
that he may be unaware that he is being destroyed. The same can be
true of love – the mutual love of two people is still too little to be
protected from mutual exploitation as a means to an end.
On 4 July 1958, during a kayaking holiday in Mazuria, when he was
discussing the manuscript of his *Love and Responsibility* with
a group of Lublin ethics scholars, "Uncle" Wojtyła received the
news that Pope Pius XII has appointed him auxiliary bishop of
Cracow. His pupils cheered him and, extremely embarrassed, he
was carried by them to the bus which took him to Warsaw
where he had been summoned by the Primate of Poland, Stefan
Cardinal Wyszyński. Then he spent a long time at prayer at the
Ursuline convent in Warsaw where he always stayed.
On 28 September 1958 at Wawel Cathedral in Cracow, Karol
Wojtyła received his consecration as bishop from the hands of
Archbishop Eugeniusz Baziak. In his bishop's seal Father Wojtyła
wrote the Latin words, *Totus Tuus*. Twenty years later in his first
papal message *Urbi et Orbi*, he said, "At this very difficult hour, full
of fear, we must turn our thoughts with filial devotion to the Virgin

Mary who always lives in the mystery of Christ and exists as His Mother; and we must repeat the words *Totus Tuus* ["completely yours"] which 20 years ago, on the day of our consecration as bishop, we inscribed into our heart and seal." He was at this time the youngest member of the Polish episcopate. In Wadowice Father Zacher inscribed in the Register of Births: "28.IX.1958 consecrated bishop," and during the solemn Mass he preached a beautiful sermon for the second time by reason of his former pupil. Joy was great among his Cracow friends. In the Swieżawski family home the new bishop was embraced with love. However, for Swieżawski Karol's appointment as bishop was at the same time a loss, for the experienced professor knew that the bishop's new duties would not allow him to devote himself completely to academic work.

Now he used to go to Lublin less often, being so involved in his duties as Bishop of Cracow. The lectures in Lublin as a result became longer and the seminars more intensive. He now had a staff of assistants to help him and of them Father Tadeusz Styczeń was his right hand man. Whenever they could not meet him in Lublin his best students and assistants travelled to Cracow to visit their Professor·Bishop in quiet Kanonicza Street. It happened more and more frequently that seminars took place on the move – on the mountain paths to Mt. Turbacz, along the lanes round Nałęczów, Ojców, or Sikornik, they spent hours walking and talking. Someone took along sandwiches, someone else coffee in a thermos flask. He performed Jurek Gałkowski's wedding ceremony in a little country church in Bolimów in the Świętokrzyskie Mountains at the

extraordinary time of 7 a.m. on a Monday morning because this was
the only hour he had any time to spare. He knew all their troubles
and helped them as much as he could, and they did not find out
until after the Conclave that they did not really know very much
about "Uncle". They learned about Wadowice, his father, mother,
and brother, his interest in the theatre and his work during the
Occupation from newspaper reports. No one had been able to
persuade him to reveal this kind of information. He always
preferred to talk about other people, never about himself.
He kept having more and more to do and there were ever more and
more people connected with his interests. He met doctors,
psychiatrists, psychologists, physicists, engineers, young people,
priests, and nuns and there were conferences, retreats, pastoral
visits, sermons, and special ceremonies. As a result he had less and
less time for himself. To Professor Swieżawski he wrote on the day
or rather night of 3/4 January 1959: "Today I was invited rather
than present." Ever more often he was tired although this
conclusion can only be drawn from comments like the one above
because he never looked it, even though he slept no more than 5 or
6 hours a night.
In 1960 *Love and Responsibility* was published by the Academic
Association of the Catholic University of Lublin. It sold out
immediately and the same happened to the second printing in 1962.
It was translated into French (1965), Italian (1968), and Spanish
(1969) and was very successful although it did not lack critics.
108 According to the author's sub-heading *Love and Responsibility* was

Manor house in Żelazowa Wola, Mazovia, the birthplace of Frédéric Chopin

"A study in ethics". However, it was not concerned with philosophical ethics but rather moral theology. The theological attitude, particularly in his treatment of the essence of the Christian marriage, preceded the discussions which were to take place after the Second Vatican Council in which Bishop Karol Wojtyła was to play a significant role.

1962 abounded in important events for the Catholic Church in the world and was just as important for Bishop Wojtyła. Almost four years after his consecration as bishop he was elected vicar-capitular after the death of Archbishop Baziak on 16 June 1962.

John XXIII, "the Pope of peace and goodness", convened the Second Vatican Council, which initiated a renewal of the Church, the famous *aggiornamento*, i.e. the integration of the Church into the life of the contemporary world. Bishop Wojtyła took part in all four sessions of the Council. He was one of the initiators of the most important constitutions of the Council – the *Lumen Gentium* – The Dogmatic Constitution of the Church, which is however not so well known to the general public, and the historic *Gaudium et Spes* – The Presence of the Church in the Modern World. He sent articles and letters from the Council's debates to Poland which were published in various periodicals. Poetry inspired by the Council by "Andrzej Jawień" also appeared in print, e.g. *Shepherds and Springs, The Church, The Birth of Confessors*, and *Considerations of Fatherhood.* For eight years he used to journey to Rome to take part in the work of the Pontifical Consilium de Laicis, i.e. the Council of the Laity, which brought into existence the decrees of

The village of Kadzidło in the Kurpie region is famous for its colourful Corpus Christi processions

Vatican II concerning the Apostolate of the Laity. Professor Swieżawski worked in another commission, Iustitia et Pax, as the only Pole. These eight years in Rome linked the two men together very closely.

After the second session of the Council of 30 December 1963, the Holy Father, Pope Paul VI appointed Karol Wojtyła Archbishop of Cracow. He moved from Kanonicza Street to the spacious Bishops' Palace at no. 3, Franciszkańska Street, from which he dispelled the air of tranquillity. Franciszek Wicher, the servant at the Palace who remembers the days of Cardinal Sapieha ("I had a lot of free time in those days," he recalls) had to adapt himself to the life-style of the new tenant. The Archbishop's residence was filled with people from morning to night and the Archbishop never had his meals alone. When there was silence in the palace it was a sign that the Archbishop was not at home. At the very start he had announced that the palace had to be open to the public and was not to be a lifeless place. He got up at 5 a.m. and his characteristic ambling gait was heard along the corridor when he went off to chapel. At 7 a.m. he celebrated Holy Mass and afterwards ate breakfast with his staff. Until 11 a.m. he worked by himself. Then he held audiences until late in the afternoon. He usually had dinner with his last guests. After this there was time for a short walk in the Lasek Wolski Park, on Kościuszko Hill or in Ojców. At 7 p.m. he had supper, followed by more guests, and the lights finally went out in the palace at midnight. Only in the chapel did a light continue to burn and there the archbishop prayed. This orderly organisation was

Jasna Góra, the Paulite Monastery in Częstochowa

disturbed by the frequent departures by the Archbishop for pastoral visitations, episcopal conferences, or trips abroad. During holiday periods, particularly before and after Christmas, the palace had to put up with a positive invasion. Doctors, workers, artists, mountain farmers, physicists, children, and students were permitted to see the Archbishop all year round. Engineers, academics, "Uncle's friends" as Franciszek called them (i.e. those young friends of his who used to come to see "Uncle", first numbering 40–60 people and later almost 200 when they came with their own children), priests, and nuns. Every year their number grew. As a result the number of people today who look on him as their friend is enormous; and he had less time and more and more duties.

The story of Nowa Huta began in the first years following the Second World War when the reconstruction of the country after the grievous wounds of the war started. The construction of Nowa Huta near Cracow, an enormous steel works, Poland's largest at that time, was a necessity for a country which was being reconstructed. The steel works and the housing estates which later grew up around it also had a symbolic importance for a new era in Poland. Building was started in 1949 on the fields of the villages of Mogiła, Bieńczyce, and Mistrzejowice near Cracow. When more steel workers arrived in the new housing estates, the monastery of the Cistercian fathers in Mogiła could not ensure adequate pastoral care for the workers. The former village of Bieńczyce, which had slowly been swallowed up in the expanding steel works, had a small chapel which could accommodate barely 200 people. During feast-days and *111*

ceremonies about 20,000 believers from the nearby new housing
estates came to the chapel. Therefore, Bishop Wojtyła decided to
build a church here and during a ceremony of homage when the
prelates, canons, and parish priests of the Cracow archdiocese came to
pay their respects to the new archbishop, Archbishop Wojtyła
persuaded Father Gorzelany, the pastor of Filipowice and a splendid
organiser, to build a church in Nowa Huta. Three days after the
conclusion of the Second Vatican Council, on 11 December 1965
during an audience with Paul VI, the Pope handed Archbishop
Wojtyła and Father Gorzelany a stone from the grave of St. Peter
with the words: "Take this stone to Poland and let it be the corner
stone for a church dedicated to the Queen of Poland at Nowa
Huta." At the same time the Pope gave the first donation of
$10,000 for a successful start to the building programme. The
construction of the church began in 1967 when Karol Wojtyła was
already a cardinal.

1966 was the year of the 1000th anniversary of Polish nationhood
and Christianity in Poland. This year was a time of hard work for
the Polish episcopate and all the clergy. Archbishop Wojtyła gave
dozens of sermons, beginning at Gniezno, the first capital of the
Polish state, then the shrine of Jasna Góra in Częstochowa, Wawel
Cathedral in Cracow, and ending with the little churches in the
Carpathian foothills. In 966 the first historical ruler of Poland,
Mieszko I of the Piast dynasty, unified the majority of the Polish
lands and after his marriage to the Bohemian princess Dąbrówka,
was baptised. Straight after the Conclave, Pope John Paul II said to

Procession during the Marian celebrations at Jasna Góra

the Archbishop of Prague, Cardinal Tomašek: "We Poles are particularly grateful to you Bohemians for the establishment of the Christian faith in Poland. In fact it was the first Slav bishop, St. Adalbert, and Princess Dąbrówka who laid this foundation. You are the successor of St. Adalbert. It was through the work of the Bohemian people that today the first Slav pope stands at the head of the Church."

On 29 May 1967 the news spread through Cracow and Poland: Karol Wojtyła had been created cardinal. He was barely 47 years old and was the youngest member of the College of Cardinals at that time. In Wadowice Father Zacher added under the name of Wojtyła in the Register of Births "*cardinalis presbiter nominatus*" and once again had the opportunity to give a solemn sermon. Two weeks later, the newly appointed cardinal participated in the oral doctoral examination of his pupil Jerzy Gałkowski, in his capacity as supervisor, at the Catholic University of Lublin. On occasion like this the Ph.D. candidate is always the hero, but this time all eyes were on the Cardinal. However, his appointment did not change him at all. When he received his cardinal's hat in Rome, one of his old fellow pupils from Wadowice high school was with him. When the newly created Cardinal was receiving congratulations, his old colleague, made formal by the dignity of the occasion, started his own congratulations with the words, "Your eminence" but he was unable to finish as the Cardinal stopped him: "Jurek, have you taken leave of your senses?" He was still direct, warm-hearted, kind, and even more surrounded by people and had even less time.

He had a table and lamp fitted in his car and spent each journey
working. Professor Swieżawski compared the cardinal to Avicenna,
the 11th century Persian philosopher who had a litter arranged for
work attached to four camels, or to Leibniz who had his carriage
fitted out in the same way.

Karol Wojtyła trained himself in yet another skill which fascinated
some and depressed others, i.e. during meetings with the staff
of *Tygodnik Powszechny*, academic seminars, lectures and symposia,
and even when he was spending evenings with friends, he always
had piles of literature and letters in his hand, and he read
continuously, regardless of whether anyone was saying anything or
not. This disconcerted those who did not know the Cardinal, who
thought that he was not listening to them and slighting them.
However he amazed them during subsequent discussions when
he gave evidence that he had followed everything exactly. He had
simply developed an extraordinary ability to divide his attention.
He continued as head of the Department of Ethics at the Catholic
University of Lublin although he could only perform the job from
Cracow. Father Styczeń, whom Cardinal Wojtyła encouraged in his
Ph.D. and post-doctoral work, took his classes in Lublin. Father
Styczeń made preparations for the Cracow seminars in Lublin and
worked out which of the theology students had to prepare papers or
summarize books and articles containing the latest ideas in ethics at
the meetings with their Professor. During these seminars, called "a
full day's work" by the participants, Dr Andrzej Szostek recalls, the
Cardinal "x-rayed" their knowledge. Frequently they left these

seminars late at night but in a state of intellectual excitement. The Cardinal did not loiter over details but attacked the heart of the matter and wrestled with it. It troubled him that the spirit of the philosophical concepts of St. Thomas Aquinas was made somewhat one-sided through his objectivism, underestimating as it were the area of consciousness and subjectivity which modern philosophy had developed. It was the Cardinal's wish to find a modern interpretation of Thomistic ideas.

In fact his second well-known book, *Osoba i czyn (The Acting Person)* written in 1968, is a further attempt to link various philosophical trends constructively, for he had always been looking for a *iunctum* between the various philosophical schools. On the other hand he writes, "Above all we strive to understand the human individual for himself". The book is not only of value for specialists, theologians and philosophers, but for anyone who is looking for his place in society. It shows that a human individual is the only author and basis of standards for moral actions. For this reason the book enlightens people, the subject of all actions, how they should become individuals and how they should protect themselves from self-destruction.

In spite of the enormous number of his duties during his period as Cardinal Karol Wojtyła had over forty academic publications to his credit, including three books. He was regarded as an unbelievably hard-working man of incredible ability. His pupils had reason for being so proud of their "Master". Writing an M.A. dissertation, not to mention a Ph.D., under his supervision was regarded as an

During a pastoral visit to Kamień Opolski

Frombork, celebrations connected with the 500th anniversary of the birth of Nicolaus Copernicus

extremely difficult task. "It's not good enough yet – carry on working on it," is what he usually said after reading a thesis draft. When he finally told people that their work was good, they knew that it really was good. Writing a Ph.D. was but one of the steps to becoming the Cardinal's academic assistant. Father Styczeń says that there were three steps although the sequence of climbing them could be different. The ideal assistant had to do his Ph.D., learn German, and be able to ski. Jerzy Gałkowski knew German, did his Ph.D., but could not ski, just like Father Andrzej Szostek. Gałkowski however vindicated himself by playing volley-ball and kayaking. Szostek could not even do these but he was the youngest of the group of assistants and did not even have his oral examination for his Ph.D. before his supervisor became Pope. This oral exam was connected with an interesting sequence of events. In July 1978 Father Szostek sent his typed thesis to the Cardinal requesting him to read it. However Pope Paul VI died and before his departure for the funeral the Cardinal just had time to write a one-page letter in which he praised Szostek and said there was no doubt that the thesis could be presented. He also wrote that he (the Cardinal) had learned a lot from it which was the greatest compliment possible for Father Szostek. In this letter the Cardinal also suggested an examination date of 11 November, but 16 October intervened. And the Pope did not forget his doctoral student. Among the thousands of other things he had to do he found time to send a letter to the Dean of the Faculty of Christian Philosophy of the Catholic University of Lublin asking that the private letter

which he had written earlier to Father Szostek should be regarded as a review of the Ph.D. as at the present time he was not able to write anything else. Thus for the first time in the history of the Catholic University of Lublin a private letter became an academic review.

However, the perfect assistant was Father Tadeusz Styczeń. He had passed his post-doctoral exams, learned several foreign languages, and also knew how to ski very well. Everyone was jealous of him because he could spend more time than anyone else with the Master. The Cardinal devoted his entire spare time to the seminars but they had to be peripatetic seminars – hiking in summer and skiing in winter. And because winters in Poland are quite long, Father Styczeń gained the most profit from this. Usually they would go to Zakopane and stay with their friends, the Ursuline sisters, in Jaszczurówka. Along the furrowed snow tracks they changed roles and here Father Styczeń was the Master. However in deep snow, even on the steep slopes of Mount Kopa Kondracka, only the Cardinal could execute a perfect Christiania turn as his assistant could not manage it. Also in mountain climbing Father Styczeń was behind, for the Cardinal, although the older of the two, had an iron constitution and was very hardy. He even preferred to go up mountains than down them. Often they skiied to Mount Turbacz although it took almost six hours to get to the top. He did not like ski trails which had lots of people on them but relaxed best of all when they were alone. Often a close friend of the Cardinal went with them, Jerzy Ciesielski, an engineer and his first skiing

instructor. When the weather was so bad that even the ski-lifts were not working, the Cardinal used to say to Father Styczeń, "Tadziu, there won't be anybody on the mountain today, let's go and try it" and Tadziu would try and defend himself but three or four times he yielded to his entreaties. Then the two of them would set off in that terrible weather up Mount Kasprowy. The wind overwhelmed them especially in the passes between the mountains and they held on to stones because the snow swept over them, and the wind whipped at them lying there. He relaxed at such times and when he returned he was completely changed. The last time they went skiing together was in March 1978 and they had planned to go again in December the same year but, as we all know, an important event intervened. In 1968 the papal encyclical *Humanae Vitae* appeared which generally speaking opposed abortion as a result of which a wave of opposition was created. Cardinal Wojtyła wrote an enormous theological and pastoral commentary on *Humanae Vitae* in which he decisively defended "unborn life". In his Cracow Chancery a department called "Centre for Family Pastoral" was established, the basis for it being contained in *Love and Responsibility*. This Department deals with religious instruction for married couples and families and is also concerned with the preparation of young Catholics for marriage and help for families with many offsprings. It in fact covers all people who need help regardless of creed. There is also a Family Institute active in the Chancery, which provides general instruction on other matters, beginning with medical problems and ending with theological ones. The Department has also carried out

the "SOS" campaign for several years which brings help to single mothers and unborn children.

In 1972, on the 900th anniversary of Stanislaus of Szczepanów being made bishop of Cracow, Cardinal Wojtyła instituted the lengthy Synod of the Cracow Archdiocese to be completed in May 1979 on the 900th anniversary of the death of Stanislaus. The aim of the Synod was "the basic adoption by the Church of the great wealth of learning stemming from the Second Vatican Council".

A vast work by Cardinal Wojtyła entitled *The Foundations of Renewal – a Study of the Realisation of the Second Vatican Council* published in 1972, showed the way for the work of the Synod. The Synod was supposed to lead the Cracow church in the post-Vatican II *aggiornamento* but did not have to erase everything which had been achieved over the centuries. It was on Cardinal Wojtyła's initiative that research was started on one of his predecessors, Bishop Stanislaus of Cracow. The martyrdom of St. Stanislaus had been a subject of controversy since the end of the 19th century. There are different interpretations of what history and legend have passed down to us as to what had happended in the 11th century. On 11 April 1079 in the Church on the Rock in Cracow, Bishop Stanislaus was killed on the orders of Boleslaus the Bold, King of Poland. It is possible that the murder was committed by the king himself although there is no evidence for it. The bishop's murder was the direct cause of the fall of the king who, banished from the country by his subjects, died in isolation in Hungary in 1081, while shortly after Bishop Stanislaus was recognised as a martyr of the

Ceremony in Auschwitz connected with the Beatification of Father Maximilian Kolbe

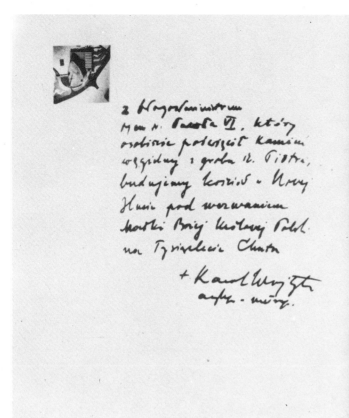

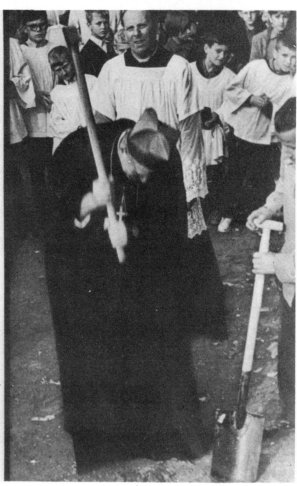

faith and in 1253 was canonised by Pope Innocent IV. But why was Stanislaus killed? This fact has been interpreted in various ways and unfortunately there is a lack of any written sources from the time of the murder; those which have been preserved come from a later date. The first person to write about this event was Gallus Anonymous, a Polish chronicler, in around 1113. Later Wincenty Kadłubek at the end of the 12th century and Jan Długosz in the 15th century also discussed it. These reports however were at least second hand and were normally written at someone's request and therefore do not always correspond to the truth. Thus the dispute between the king and the bishop should be examined not so much on the basis of the above-mentioned sources as on the basis of our knowledge of contemporary history. One of the reasons for the conflict between the two men who initially were linked by friendship (In 1076 Boleslaus had received the crown of Poland from the hands of Pope Gregory VII, the same man to whom a year later the Emperor Henry IV was forced to submit at Canossa – this was the period of the wars between the Empire and the Papacy) was the increasingly tyrannical rule and debauched way of living of Boleslaus which Stanislaus by reason of his office was forced to attack. The dispute certainly lasted for several years and each side used ever more powerful arguments. The king proclaimed the bishop a traitor (once again there is a lack of any evidence as to why) and then he brought an action against him for his knightly estates which he was supposed to have acquired in a manner not in keeping with the law. Then Stanislaus, in what is supposed to be the

Karol Cardinal Wojtyła during the ceremony of laying the foundation stone for the church in Nowa Huta in Cracow

final stage of the dispute, is said to have excommunicated the king
and this resulted in the sentence of "severing of the limbs" passed
on the bishop. Nine years after his death, his body, which had
originally been buried in St. Michael's Church, was solemnly
transferred to Wawel Cathedral which already then was the
honoured place of rest for the most distinguished Poles. So much for
facts and suppositions. It is difficult to form an unequivocal
judgment on the basis of this material but thanks to the initiative of
Cardinal Wojtyła historians at least managed to establish some
essential facts which at the present state of our knowledge do not
allow us to form an explicit interpretation of these events.
Historians were not the only group of academics with whom the
Archbishop of Cracow maintained contact. Cracow's academic
circles occupied a particular place among his activities. As an
academic he knew the worries and troubles of this milieu. Thanks to
him several interesting schemes were undertaken by many famous
scholars. "I regarded him as a patron of learning," said the
physicist, Professor Zygmunt Chyliński, later, "when for the first
time he organised a symposium devoted to the natural sciences at
his home on Franciszkańska Street, dealing especially with the role
of physics in the great debate on knowledge. Many other famous
Cracow scholars also took part in this seminar, including the late
Professors Ingarden, Weyssenhoff, Gierula and Czyżewski, and
many other experts from all over Poland who are well-known today.
Similar symposia at the Bishops' Palace were attended by lawyers,
economists, doctors, and chemists, for example the psychiatrist

The modern church building was blended into the landscape of a huge housing development

Antoni Kępiński, the legal historian Adam Vetulani, the Polish literature historian Stanisław Pigoń, the physicist Henryk Niewodniczański, the haematologist Julian Aleksandrowicz, the historian Aleksander Gieysztor, the economist Edward Lipiński, and the botanist Franciszek Górski. The Cardinal's residence became a veritable centre of academic learning.

The building of the church in Nowa Huta started on 14 October 1967 when at 7 a.m. the Cardinal arrived at the town. He celebrated Holy Mass, seized a pick-axe and heaved it a couple of times, and then dug the first section of a trench in the foundations with a spade. After him the pastor, the assistants, and the faithful started digging. And from that day onwards every day came hundreds of people, dressed in their Sunday best, not as if they had come to work but as if they had come to a church which did not yet exist and which they were in fact building. The Cardinal was interested in every detail of the construction and often turned up uninvited and unexpected, eating somewhere nearby afterwards. He chatted with the pastor, the workers, and the engineers. He blessed them and carried on. Groups of seminarians, monks and young people from university came from all over Poland to work on the church for one or two days or even weeks. Also international groups of young people came under the sign of a symbol of penance called the *Sühnezeichen,* as well as from the Belgian organisation "Bauorden". These young people worked during their holidays on the Nowa Huta church in the spirit of the idea of payment for the crimes perpetrated by the Nazis on Polish territory. They worked,

The consecration of the church in Nowa Huta

The church in Nowa Huta, designed
by Wojciech Pietrzyk
Interior with crucifix sculpture
by Bronisław Chromy

played and relaxed together. In the evenings during discussions
which were conducted by the editors of *Tygodnik Powszechny* they
talked about ecumenism, reconciliation, Poland and the world. The
Cardinal himself liked to come and visit these young people very
much. He was straightforward, without any reserve, and even
shocked them because in their countries they only saw bishops in
state and at a distance. On the other hand here was a bishop who
laughed, told jokes, and also spoke very wisely. It makes one
wonder how they received the news that he had been made Pope.
The Cardinal took part in every important moment during the
building of the church. With his own hands he placed the corner
stone in the wall, dedicated the walls, and was present at the placing
of the roof, and the raising of the cross. Finally on 15 May 1977 the
church was consecrated. The Cardinal loved the Nowa Huta church
and later would often return to it, and although it was not the only
church which had been built on his initiative, this one had
a particular importance for him.

One of the most beloved places in Karol Wojtyła's life ever since he
had been a small boy was Kalwaria Zebrzydowska with its 17th
century Bernardine monastery, its exquisite church, and its famous
picture of Our Lady and the Roads to Calvary (*Kalwaria* in
Polish). Time and again he used to come over from Cracow, even
for a couple of hours, to be able to talk to the Almighty in peace
and quiet. Kalwaria had everything he most desired – the rolling
Beskid Mountains covered with forests, tranquillity, and a place for
worship immortalised by tradition. Here on one of the Roads (there

127

is a cluster of 44 churches and chapels scattered over a 6 km. area
here with its own particular topographical and architectural layout
recalling the holy places in Jerusalem and with pilgrims flocking
here in large numbers holding processions) he would often set off
alone regardless of the weather, whether in rain, or on skis in the
winter, and pray. Here he used to say, "I consign to Thee the
Church of Cracow in its entirety – priests, religious communities,
families, parents, young people, children, pastoral centres; here
I consign to Thee all the troubles of the church and I always hope
that this bishop's prayer will be mixed with the prayers of all people
who pray here that they may come together and form one whole."
Thanks to him Kalwaria became the centre of the religious life of
the diocese. He was here on the 20th anniversary of being
consecrated bishop but he did not spend the day receiving
congratulations and best wishes but on the Roads to Calvary and in
a monk's cell – for him this was a day of retreat. A few hours after
the Cardinal's last departure from Kalwaria Pope John Paul I died.
The 1970's were a time of continual foreign trips for Cardinal
Wojtyła, with congresses, academic symposia, and pastoral visits
which took him to his countrymen scattered all over the world, in
Canada, USA, Australia, New Guinea, New Zealand, and
Tasmania. The enthusiastic welcomes and the unique atmosphere of
encounters remained for a long time in the memory of everybody
and especially of the Poles who were far-distant from their native
land. On the other hand academic trips brought Cardinal Wojtyła

recognition among the world's theologians and philosophers.

The Grand Congress on Thomistic Studies in Rome and Naples in 1974, organised to celebrate the 700th anniversary of the death of St. Thomas Aquinas, in which almost 2,000 scholars from all over the world participated, was called "the Congress of Cardinal Wojtyła" in the Conference lobbies. He was the leading personality of the Congress and not only because he was the only cardinal present. He gave one of the main introductory papers on the subject of man's problems in connection with his book *The Acting Person* and the paper was enthusiastically received. After the round table discussions the whole greatness of the learned cardinal from Poland in matters of theology and philosophy became apparent. Poles taking part in the Congress were even a little surprised by the enthusiasm shown by those present and were completely shocked when they heard from them that Karol Wojtyła was *papabilis*, i.e. had a chance of becoming Pope. Halfway through the debates the participants went by coach from Rome to Naples and stopped on the way for lunch. While waiting they formed into various language groups. The Cardinal went from one group of people to another, sat on the arms of chairs, asked questions, and cracked jokes. He also went over to a group that included Jerzy Gałkowski, started talking, clapped one of them on the back and smiled at another, and when he had gone away, some of the Swiss present asked Gałkowski who the man was, for they could not know as the work of the Congress had been carried out in several groups working on different problems. Gałkowski replied that he was a professor from his university, Cardinal Wojtyła. They could hardly

believe him for how could he be a cardinal if he was dressed in
a black cassock, sat on the arms of chairs, and clapped people on
the back? "It's impossible," said one of them, "he is behaving just
like an ordinary man!" Later there was a famous mass in the Fossa
Nuova where St. Thomas Aquinas had died and here Cardinal
Wojtyła gave a magnificent sermon on the two Thomases, the
Apostle and the Philosopher. Hearing this sermon, Professor
Swieżawski thought for the first time that the Cardinal possessed all
the talents necessary to become Pope. After the service he told him
this directly and on the Saturday 21 October 1978 the day before
his inauguration as Pope in a hand-written letter to Professor
Swieżawski John Paul II wrote, "...Yes, dear Stefan, I remember
those words of yours in the Fossa Nuova... and I thank you for your
constant goodwill which has gone with me for years ...and I'm very
much counting on it that it will continue to go with me for much
longer. The test awaiting me will certainly be greater than any
I have experienced so far in my life..."
In February 1976 Cardinal Wojtyła was invited to the Vatican by
Pope Paul VI to deliver 22 lectures in retreats. Apart from the Holy
Father cardinals, bishops, prelates, and members of the Pope's
household took part in these retreats. These lectures were published
in Italian and Polish under the title of *The Sign of Contradiction*.
These retreats were really a major appeal for the permanent
testimony of truth for God and Man.
It is difficult to know what else should be added to the story of

Karol Wojtyła. He was the chairman of the Commission for

On the following pages:
Snapshots from Karol
Cardinal Wojtyła's
foreign visits

Catholic Education and of the Commission for the Lay Apostolate
of the Polish Episcopate. In 1977 he received the degree of *doctor
honoris causa* from the Gutenberg University of Mainz, etc., etc....
It in fact seemed that this was the climax of the honours and praise
which Cardinal Wojtyła had attained.

Monsignor Kazimierz Figlewicz, pastor of Cracow's Wawel Cathedral,
learned of the election of Cardinal Wojtyła as Pope from the 7 p.m.
news on the radio. The old man's hands were shaking with
excitement when he received telephone calls from all over the city.
There were insistent questions of "Why don't you ring the bells?"
"Why is the 'Sigismund' bell in the Wawel not ringing?" "Why is
the church closed?" The clergy of the Chapter gathered together to
make sure that the news was true. Crowds of people thronged to the
Wawel gates although everywhere was closed because the Wawel
was locked at 5 p.m. in autumn. The gates and Cathedral were
opened against regulations. Students came from the nearby
seminary and the Cathedral was filled with the inhabitants of
Cracow. Before 9 p.m. "Sigismund" was resounding and after it the
bells of all the churches started ringing in a harmonious chorus.
Some say that the bells started ringing first of all in Dębniki in the
Church of St. Stanislaus Kostka but it is said in Cracow that until
"Sigismund" starts ringing nothing of any great importance has
taken place. But something of importance had taken place for this
was Monday 16 October 1978.
Cracow which is usually quiet and sleepy at this time of day was

alive. Joyful and enthusiastic crowds of people flooded into the
Market Place. Nuns were seen dancing in the street. A photograph
of the Cardinal was placed on the pedestal of the monument to
Adam Mickiewicz and flowers were seen, in Kanonicza Street in
front of the former residence of the Cardinal, on Franciszkańska
Street in front of the Bishops' Palace, and in front of the Podwale
theological seminary. "Habemus Papam". "We, the Poles, have
a Pope!" "A Pope of our own who grew up on our joys and
sorrows". A Pope whom Juliusz Słowacki foretold at the beginning
of the 19th century:

> Among conflicting mortals the Almighty
> strikes a huge bell
> And has prepared the Papal throne
> for a Slav Pope...
> Now here he comes, the new giver of strength
> for the whole world...
> And he puts an end to power and
> lifts up the Earth...
> Yes, here he comes, a Slav Pope,
> People's brother...
> He spreads love as the mighty
> dispense their arms,
> He reveals the power of the sacrament
> Joining mankind together...

At midnight Wawel Cathedral echoed with joyful hymns and
a service of thanksgiving was celebrated.

In Wadowice, the family parish of the Polish Pope, the result of the Conclave was known immediately. Evening mass was being held at that very moment when Canon Zdzisław Kałwa, his voice faltering, announced the news from the altar to the faithful. The church was hushed and a second later there was an explosion of joy and tears. The Dean of Wadowice, Father Edward Zacher, also broke down in tears and shouted with joy, "But he did not keep his word, he did not keep his word". The priests kissed one another and the little town echoed with noise and the bells started ringing. About 8 p.m. there was a telephone call from the British Embassy requesting an interview for the BBC. The first British journalist was travelling down to Wadowice that same evening. Father Zacher, a 75 year old man, staggered around the brightly-lit rectory, waved his stick, and kept bellowing, "He did not keep his word". With trembling hands he opened the thick, well-worn Register of Births and on page 549, under the name Karol Wojtyła, wrote, "*ad summum pontificatum electus et imposuit sibi nomen Johannes Paulus secundus*" (elected to the highest office of the Church and chose for himself the name John Paul II). The old pastor had never thought that he would one day have to write such an entry. "But he did not keep his word," he repeated. The meaning of this strange phrase was that when Father Zacher gave his fifth sermon in honour of his former pupil, during celebrations of the 50th anniversary of his christening, he had told the Cardinal at that time that there was only one more sermon like this left for him to say – when the Cardinal became Pope. The latter first of all grunted and then said that there would never be a sixth

sermon, "And he didn't keep his word for the first time in his life,"
said Father Zacher.

On the Tuesday morning reporters came flooding into Wadowice –
Paris Match, Stern, reporters and commentators from Rome, Milan,
Bonn and also Polish ones from the radio and television, and
journalists from the weeklies and the dailies. They descended on the
rectory and gathered around Father Zacher, climbing on to chairs
and tables, kneeling, sitting on the floor, and asking dozens of
questions. The priest agreed to everything and said "All right"
because that was the only thing he could say in English. "Did you
like him?" they asked. "He was my pupil for six years. I taught him.
He's the one who should like me, not vice versa," laughed the old
priest. They asked about everything and he had to give answers.

In front of the little glass-case which had been knocked together in
a hurry at the entrance to the catechetic centre there stood small
groups of people. In the case was a picture of John Paul II from his
youth and one from the last time he had visited his birthplace.
People stopped and wandered down the lane and looked in the
window of the presbytery and came into the religious instruction
room. This had been the Church Hall before the war and here,
almost 40 years before, the teenage "Lolek" had acted in the
theatre group led by Father Zacher. People came into the large hall
where there were rows of chairs and a stage. In the two front rows
in their blue overalls were some young children with a priest in front
of them having a catechism class. Behind the priest was the stage,
just like it had been years before. Not much had changed; probably

only the fact that now catechism classes and services took place
here because there was an altar placed on the stage.
Down the lane by the church came cars belonging to French
Television. Young children with flushed cheeks were running along
the walls and adults were standing around in groups, watching,
wondering, and making comments. Fate had smiled on Wadowice.
The late-Baroque church was decorated with papal flags and a large
portrait of the Cardinal. Usually quiet in the morning, it was filled
to overflowing with people and had candles burning and bunches of
flowers in front of the beautiful Baroque font. Lost in thought
people stood on the very spot where 58 years before a month-old
infant had been christened Carolus Joseph. People knew this and
this is what is said on a tablet inserted into the wall in 1970 during
the ceremony to mark the 50th anniversary of the baptism – "To
our great countryman we dedicate this tablet," the citizens of
Wadowice had inscribed at that time. Is this where one should look
for the origins of the Pontificate of Karol Wojtyła? "Of course,"
said Canon Zdzisław Kałwa, "When we had the 50th anniversary
celebrations here," he added, "the Cardinal stood for a long time in
silence in front of the font and then walked through the whole
church without trappings of office in complete humility like a child.
I saw him myself – like a child, yes just like a child – that's the right
word – like a child of God." At the side altar, in front of the picture
of Our Lady of Perpetual Help there were also flowers and people.
This was the place where he had usually prayed, right from the time
he was a small child to recent years. Sometimes, when he was

passing through, he did not even enter the rectory but always came here if only for a few minutes.

Near the church, on the opposite side of the road from the rectory, there was a crowd of people standing. In the modest little house at no. 7, Kościelna Street, just like most of the houses in Wadowice, Karol Wojtyła had been born and lived until he was 18. People went into the building, up the metal spiral staircase to the first floor. There was a landing here, shared by several families, which led off to separate flats. Here everyone knows one another and knows everything about each other just as they did years ago. There is a large room with two windows, a second smaller room, and a tiny kitchen – almost the same as it had been years before. Now the Putyra family lives here. Zbigniew Putyra, a teacher at the local high school, had been late for classes the previous day for he had been besieged by newspaper reporters. They filmed him, they asked him questions, and when they learned that he had known Wojtyła since their school days, they would not leave him alone. Yes, he knew him, and they had even gone to the same high school together, but Putyra had been two years his junior. Putyra had often seen the Wojtyłas, father and son, when they went for walks. He knew that they had dinner on the other side of the street at "Banaś's" restaurant which does not exist any more.

In front of the church on Armii Czerwonej Square, there were crowds of Wadowice citizens. TV and film cameras hovered over the crowd and zoomed in on them. "Who knew the Pope?" shouted

Anthony Halik, a Polish-American famous for his interesting

reports. A forest of hands went up and he chose one of them –
wisely, as it turned out, because it belonged to Zenon Kęcki, the
former gymnastics and soccer coach of the prewar Sokół club. Yes,
Wojtyła used to play soccer at Mikołajka where there is a stadium
today; he liked to play and in fact he played reasonably well as
goal-keeper – something which surprised the American camera
men. Some reporters from Associated Press plied the stationary
crowd with copies of the latest edition of *Tygodnik Powszechny* with
a large picture-spread on the life of the Pope. The people had to
read them and the cameramen filmed them. And so the show went
on in the reborn, revitalised small town of Wadowice with
a population of barely 15,000 which the whole world now knew
about.

The mayor of Wadowice and district had been late in switching on
his TV that Monday evening. At that very moment there was
a picture of a building which he did not associate with Rome. At the
end he heard the voice of the newsreader saying that Karol Wojtyła
had been made Pope. He thought it was a joke and did not believe
it until he heard the news again on the radio. What a sensation!
Immediately he knew that thousands of people would descend on
Wadowice and he was annoyed that there were no brochures about
the town for they were being printed at the time. His office would
have to get them ready, for the invasions were about to begin. Each
package group from abroad would want to see the Pope's birthplace. Foreign correspondents who visited the councillor were most
of all interested in how many churches there were in Wadowice and

137

he told them that there were five for 15,000 inhabitants, the same ratio as for Rome – "which is why a Holy Father from Wadowice has been chosen," laughed the mayor.

The economics graduate Zbigniew Siłkowski lives on Czerwonej Armii Square over the chemist's. A tall, strong man, full of dignity, he bore the invasion of journalists with equanimity. Yes, he was a friend of the man whom everyone was now talking about. Their friendship dated back to their schooldays and still continued till the present time. They had studied together, gone on outings together, played soccer and acted in plays together. Their whole class had formed a close-knit intimate group and had kept up reunions until the present time. As Karol's duties increased, he had had less and less time for his old friends. It happened that, when they said goodbye in Wadowice, before he gave a farewell wave through the open window of his car, he had already opened his collapsible table, switched on the small lamp, and got down to work. In May that year they were supposed to meet for the 40th anniversary of their school-leaving examination. The reunion, however, had not taken place but the two of them had met, albeit under different circumstances. Cardinal Wojtyła had conducted the funeral service for his friend's wife. When Zbigniew Siłkowski learned of Karol's election on that October Monday, he embraced his children and was unable to hold back his tears. As well as rejoicing there was also sadness that Karol had taken such a heavy burden on himself. He was sorry for his friend whom he would probably never see again, or maybe just once more when he went to Rome – maybe. "I've

probably already lost him," he stammered through his tears. "I realise that, but I shall go to Rome to say goodbye to him." After a moment of silence he added, as if to himself, "What have I contributed to his life? I don't know. He is the kind of man who does not remain indifferent to another human being."

In the Emil Zegadłowicz High School in Wadowice no record has remained of school-leavers beyond the year 1938. During the Occupation a German school had been housed here and all Polish records were destroyed by the Nazis. Only one thing has been preserved – just the record of the school year 1937/8 in which there is a list of names of the school-leavers with Karol Józef Wojtyła at number 38. The high school is over 100 years old, with large, broad corridors and acres of classrooms. The building is the same although its atmosphere has changed somewhat and it now has the name of Emil Zegadłowicz and not Marcin Wadowita High School. For the present headmaster of the school, Tadeusz Janin, the most famous son of Wadowice is now the Pope. "We are the only non-Italian school which can claim the honour of having such a pupil," he says movingly. In the classes held that day and the day before the pupils had bombarded their teachers with dozens of questions, especially those teachers who had known Wadowice before the war.

Lublin on that Monday evening was a city of joy and excitement. After the first TV announcement, students from the Catholic University of Lublin crowded out of their hall of residence on Sławińskiego Street and marched in procession with banners and singing songs through the whole of the city to the academic church

American bishops in Poland

with passers-by joining the procession on the way. The telephone
never stopped ringing at the Gałkowski household and more than
a dozen people came to his home where Dr Gałkowski uncorked
the best wine which he had been saving for his wife's post-
doctoral exam. Professor Jerzy Kłoczowski, the historian, brought
some French champagne which he had been keeping for New Year.
They made up a joint telegram to be sent to the Vatican and sat far
into the night, chatting. Halina Bortnowska, *Tygodnik Powszechny*
reporter, said later, "During these days Poles were engaged in two
activities – praying and reminiscing". In Lublin the cheers lasted
until dawn and the building of the Catholic University was
decorated with flags and banners saying "Our Professor the Pope".
At 3 p.m. an extraordinary ceremonial sitting of the University
Senate took place which decided to strike a special medal to
commemorate the election of a Catholic University professor as
Pope. It was also decided that the Holy Father should be the first
person to receive the medal "for services to the Catholic University
of Lublin", struck on the occasion of the 60th anniversary of the
University. A large group of university students and staff made
preparations for their trip to Rome to the enthronement of the
Pope. The University, although used to journalists by now, went
through a veritable invasion by them and academic staff,
particularly those from the Department of Ethics, gave dozens of
interviews. Reporters dug up all the photos of the Holy Father in
the University archive and the head of the publishing department of
the University was inundated with telegrams from abroad with

141

The Marian sanctuary in Kalwaria Zebrzydowska

requests for the dispatch of articles and books by Professor Karol Wojtyła.

It is not possible to read in records the date when Karol Wojtyła started work at the Solvay plant in Cracow because such records do not exist any more. There are only the people who remember him and the factory itself which still produces lime today, albeit by different methods. Franciszek Dyrga has been working in the quarries for 41 years and has an astonishing memory. He and Karol used to go together by narrow-gauge railway to Borek for the soup for the workers in the quarry. I looked at Dyrga's hands which are thickly-veined and knotted with exhaustion. When they sat in the jolting waggons Karol also complained that his hands hurt him terribly although he did not have the hardest work. He did not break rocks with a hammer but shovelled away the bits left over from the quarrying. "Let us go to the bottom of the large quarry. He most often worked here, but a little higher, and here," Dyrga indicated, "was the ledge which is now grown over with weeds." The memory of Wojtyła's stay here lingers on. Quickly and unexpectedly "the student" was transferred from the quarry to the factory. It was not only he but everybody at Solvay looked for an escape from the worst jobs. He started in the boiler room – Jan Wilk remembers him from there. When they sat down to breakfast – Włosiński, Sieprawski, Orawczyk, and Wilk – they shared their breakfast with him. Then he was transferred from the boiler-room to the other sections – the foundry, crystallisation department, and

caustic section. Adam Dyras remembers him from there when he

was head of department: "He did all kinds of manual labour and
disappeared from sight in 1944 and I didn't see him again until his
consecration as bishop because he sent me an invitation. Once,
a couple of years later, I was looking out of the window of my house
opposite the factory and I saw a car stop. I recognized him. He
opened the window and looked at the factory for about 15 minutes
and then he closed the window and carried on in his car."
Niegowić is a small village. The entire parish of five villages scarcely
numbers 5,000 inhabitants. Very little has changed here except
perhaps·for some new houses, an asphalt road, and a new church.
The old wooden church where the young Father Wojtyła used to
perform his office as curate, was taken down and transferred
elsewhere and a new larger church of stone was erected. Building
was started in 1949 after the arrival of the young priest. I looked
through the Register of Baptisms, Births, Marriages, and Deaths
from the years 1948 and 1949, trying to find traces of the work of
Father Wojtyła. Everything had been recorded, even who had
performed what duties. His first baptism – Barbara Filipkowska, 22
November 1948; his first wedding – Stanisław Substelny and Józefa
Strojna from the village of Marszowice, 20 October 1948, both of
whom are still alive and live in the same place. They have a little
house, not much space, and are already quite old and wrinkled and
not the same as they were in their wedding photograph but they still
have good memories. What was the wedding like? "Ordinary,
nothing special. He didn't come to the reception after the wedding
because he wasn't invited. Perhaps it was for the best that he didn't   *143*

Cracow's Old Town
Market Square with
the Church of Our Lady

come because there was some shooting – those were the days just
after the war. He brought luck to our marriage. Everything has gone
well for us. I'm sure he doesn't remember us, all those years ago,
but we haven't forgotten. It must be hard for him to be so far away,
not among his own people any more."
Foreign newspaper reporters found their way to Niegowić. The
pastor there, Father Józef Gąsiorowski, has recently had the
vicarage redecorated, the same vicarage where Father Wojtyła used
to live. In the window of one of the rooms are some flowers and
a large portrait of Cardinal Wojtyła. Father Gąsiorowski has
a splendid memory of the Cardinal's old, battered, worn-out hat. "I
think he was even a bit ashamed of it when he used to come to the
parish. He would drop in and ask, 'How are you getting along,
Józef?' He enjoyed a good joke and made me give a different story
each time. He made me afraid that he wouldn't come again if
I didn't crack some jokes. He had a way of putting you at your ease.
'We'll have a quick bite to eat – anything will do for me – and I'm
away.' Now, when I see him in the Sistine Chapel, tears come into
my eyes."
Papal flags are flying from the church in Niegowić. In front of the
church are cars with various national registrations and groups of
people. People are busy getting ready for their departure for Rome.
The parish priest is not going as he has been there three times
before and he is sending two assistants instead so that they can see
the inauguration.

144   Cracow, on Sunday 22 October before 10 a.m., the time for the

Wawel Cathedral in Cracow

start of the live broadcast from the Vatican, is like a dead city; buses and even trams are not halting at request stops because there is no one getting on or getting off. There are feelings of pride, joy, wonder, and perhaps sadness mixed with apprehension because this man, our Polish Peter, perhaps would also like to be elsewhere just like that first Peter wanted to stay on the Sea of Galilee.

What the Polish Press Said

Słowo Powszechne (17 October 1978): "Not only have the great personal qualities of the man raised to the throne of St. Peter been honoured but also the whole 1,000 years of the tradition of Polish Christianity – its constantly living, profound, and earnest faith and its strong links with the soil of Poland and the fate of the nation. In celebrating the great jubilee of the 1000 years of Christianity in Poland not so long ago, we certainly did not suspect that the second thousand years would start so splendidly with a Polish Cardinal as head of the Universal Church.
"The name which Karol Cardinal Wojtyła has assumed – John Paul II – is clear evidence that he will continue the line of the Pontificate of his predecessors... Continuing their programme simply means realising in practice through the whole Church the injunctions of the Second Vatican Council, meeting the needs of modern man halfway, and giving an answer to the questions which he has been addressing to the Church."

Życie Warszawy (21–22 October 1978): "If today the elevation of a Pole to the Papal throne, an event without precedent in history, has become a fact, it is difficult to evaluate this fact outside the realities which shaped the personality of priest, then bishop, and finally Cardinal Wojtyła. Certainly his elevation to the highest dignity within the Roman Catholic Church, and probably recognized as such in all Christendom, is above all the consequence of the recognition of the personal qualities of John Paul II by the College of Cardinals, his willingness to work in a place in which the burden of the responsibility he will receive is difficult to imagine. However, his personality has been formed in a concrete world under specific circumstances and therefore to some degree derived from the general increase in importance of Poland."

Cardinals Stefan Wyszyński and Karol Wojtyła on their way to the Conclave which chose John Paul I as Pope

Polityka (21 October 1978): "Habemus Papam... certainly never before has this expression had such a specific or literal ring in the ears of Polish Catholics. It means not only the standard announcement of the election of a new Pope but also the fact that Pope John Paul II, Karol Cardinal Wojtyła, is a Pole. He comes from a country whose history in many aspects is linked with the history of Catholicism and at the same time from a country which is building a socialist system – also on the basis of cooperation between Catholics and Marxists... The Pope is not only the Supreme Pontiff of the Roman Catholic Church as one of his titles says but also a leading moral authority in the modern world. The elevation of a Pole to this office is of particular importance as for 34 years

Poland has been a special example of a creative and fruitful
coexistence between non-believers and Catholics. The basis for this
coexistence has included the age-old tradition of national tolerance
in a country which has never seen religious wars or burnings at the
stake.

"The modern world requires cooperation between all people –
a genuine dialogue in fact. The Church on its side started this
dialogue with the turning-point of the Second Vatican Council,
carried out under the Pontificate of John XXIII and Paul VI, with
the opening up to the modern world. This world is so varied and
divided and at the same time has so much in common that its
further development and existence cannot be imagined without
constant regularly continued attempts at mutual understanding...
16 October 1978 was not only a solemn and important date in the
history of the Papacy but in the history of the world too. It is
difficult to grasp today all the consequences of this election for the
Church and for the world. May they be favourable for both..."

Tygodnik Powszechny (22 October 1978): "The first fact which
astonished not only us Poles but the whole world was the election of
a non-Italian as head of the Roman-Catholic Church and Bishop of
Rome. This happened for the first time after over 400 years of
a tradition which in the case of the last three Pontificates and also
many times in the past had produced great Popes for the Church
and the world. The tradition has been broken this time by the
Cardinals who have made such a choice for the sake of the need of   *147*

Monsignor Edward Zacher, pastor of Wadowice

Monsignor Kazimierz Figlewicz, pastor of Wawel Cathedral

the contemporary situation in Christendom, which had been
recognized as important by them. In this way the Church has shown
a new reality for the first time and thanks to the decisions of the
most recent Popes and the influence of the Second Vatican Council
has changed externally and structurally in the course of the last few
decades, aware, more profoundly and anew, of the general and
universal mission placed on it by Christ – 'Go and teach unto all
nations'. Therefore in our pleasure at the election of a Pole as Pope
let us bear in mind that he is the servant of all servants of God, of
the entire great commonwealth of God's mankind which belongs to
many cultures, speaks an innumerable number of different
languages, and has more than just one, European tradition of
Christianity.

"However we must feel a natural pride in the fact that the national
and Christian culture in which Cardinal Karol Wojtyła grew up and
was educated and himself helped create in his adult years, that the
Polish church within which the man who is now John Paul II has
served and performed his spiritual calling, contained and still
contains creative, intellectual and spiritual forces which enrich with
their own special characteristics and universal values, that they are
now able to serve the entire Catholic Church. 'Gaude Mater
Polonia' ('Rejoice, Mother Poland')."

Literatura (26 October 1978): "The course of world affairs often
brings with it unexpected events and surprises. However, the history
of mankind rarely surprises us with the election of a Polish cardinal

as head of the Roman Catholic Church. Therefore we have
observed this event in Poland with deeply stirred emotions. I think
that the dominant feelings among Poles have been first and
foremost pride and a patriotic feeling of satisfaction, as a kind of
recompense for the many things which our past society has
endured... The destiny of the undoubted moral authority which the
Holy See enjoys is in the hands of a Polish clergyman...
a man of great knowledge and strength of conviction whose
entire adult life was formed at a time of war which assaulted Poland
so brutally, and then under circumstances of rebuilding the country
within a socialist system. It is not possible that these events have
had no influence on his attitudes... In this way a link is established
between Poland and Italian culture with its language, art, and
literature, in the heart of which the Holy See is situated. Therefore
the new Pope went to Rome not only from a native land of bravery,
roadside shrines, Marian May services, and religious processions but
also represents a nation with great creative and multifarious
intellectual resources. Such a legacy imposes its obligations and was
taken into account in the election of a Polish cardinal... This Polish,
let us even say Slav, Pontificate, will not be an easy one. Its work
will come to be measured by particular prudence. We should also
expect a wise balancing of many interested parties for this
significant historical event to be inscribed in the history of Poland as
happy and successful, as a fruitful event for mankind. We have
considered an event which has gone all round the world and also we
have listened to what has gone on over the last few days in Rome."

Zbigniew Siłkowski, a friend since school days

Dr Jerzy Gałkowski, academic assistant of Cardinal Karol Wojtyła

Więź (December 1978): "Several months ago in the Bishops' Palace in Cracow a symposium took place dedicated to the memory of the prematurely deceased Professor Antoni Kępiński. There were both staff from the Psychiatric Clinic and representatives of the Polish Episcopate present at that time. In conversations in the lobby Cardinal Wojtyła asked me about the progress of the research by the group of which I am head on the ecological prevention of diseases which threaten the survival of mankind today. In a few warm words he indicated that he would like to take part in the work in some way because he felt the great importance which this scientific trend had for reducing human suffering. ...The explosion of joy... which we have seen is a belief that his Pontificate will contribute to the peace of the world not through arms *(si vis pacem, para bellum)* but through the rediscovery of peace itself and among all populations in the world *(si vis salutem, para pacem)*... Let us believe that Our Pope will accomplish great work in this sphere, for he is a son of the soil, of all the soils in the world, the one most imbued with the blood of its defenders and defenceless ones."

Julian Aleksandrowicz, haematologist

"...A historian cannot resist the thought that the longest-lived institution that the Holy See is can renew itself by returning to the basic idea of a Universal Church. In breaking the monopoly of one nation – that is the Italian monopoly which continued for over 450 years – which was strengthened during the time when the Church was fighting the Reformation and centralising its new institutions,

a non-Italian bishop has been appointed to the highest office in the

Franciszek Wicher and Maria Morda, servant and housekeeper respectively at the Bishops' Palace in Cracow

Zofia Poźniak

Roman Catholic Church by a brave collective decision which recognized a Pole as being most worthy of this post. Once before, though a long time ago, during a difficult crisis in the Church, there was another Polish candidate for the Papal throne. At the Council at Constance in 1417, the Archbishop of Gniezno and Primate of Poland, a kind of medieval self-made man, Mikołaj Trąba, politician and diplomat who defended the Polish raison d'etat at this international congress, won many votes for himself at the time of the Papal election, according to the trustworthy Polish historian, Jan Długosz, which were transferred to the majority candidate, the future Pope Martin V. This time there were no elements of compromise between conflicting parties but the Polish candidature formed a third solution in that it opened up the future and was based on the realisation that it is impossible to link this future either with any one particular country or with any particular political system..."

Aleksander Gieysztor, historian

"We are inclined to regard the recent Conclave as the personal success of 35 million Poles. At the same time it has imposed a double obligation on each of us – to be equal to the worthiness of a nation which has given the Church its Holy Father and to be equal in our characters to Christians, citizens and mankind's members. The new Pope knows us too well not to blush at our weaknesses. He has called upon us to pray for him. We can therefore phrase our prayers in this way – to request that he may be granted a settlement of our major problems which have been so complicated for

Professor Stefan Swieżawski and his wife

Józefa and Stanisław Substelny of Niegowić

Wadowice, 17 October 1978

Franciszek Dyrga, friend from the Solvay days

centuries. However one dominant thought should guide us – *Non nobis, sed Nomini Tuo da gloriam.*

Stefan Kieniewicz, historian

"...It is apparent that Pope John Paul II will be a Pope of compromise, that no one idea threatens him, that he will not be 'suspect' from the start, even though his person and intentions are reflected in different ways at the same time in the mirror of world opinion and press... He grew up in an atmosphere of popular Catholicism, at the same time intuitively mystical and very much connected with naive traditional representations of rural art where Christ was a wooden, sorrowing image and God had a long white beard. At the same time, however, the Cardinal from Wadowice in the Beskid foothills is a man of the world, an intellectual in debates, a professor of philosophy, a doctor of theology, and a polyglot. Who could be more suitable for compromise, for a return to a balance between extreme points of view, neither of which should be disregarded? Also with regard to matters of marriage which threw Catholic Italy into a state of confusion not so long ago the new Pope's empirical realism and his acquaintance with the life of simple people, who are not always so simple, should make sure that he will find an evangelical way out which is neither 'progressive' or 'reactionary' or doctrinal but human..."

Stefan Kisielewski, journalist

"...The world is tired of the tyranny of science, selfish interests in international relations, and strongly feels the need for these relations to acquire a moral content. Perhaps the world has always been in a crisis – a political, social or moral one. However we feel the present crisis to be a particularly difficult, particularly wide-spread, and particularly severe one. Beliefs which people lived on until recently have collapsed. Great historical experiments have proved how difficult it is to improve people's lives by techniques

155

which we once regarded as infallible. The belief that man is omnipotent and can form his own destiny in a planned way has vanished. However the hope has not vanished that the world might improve and that a better future is ahead for mankind. This is in fact a belief which we are now linking with the wonderful figure of the new Pope, John Paul II."

Edward Lipiński, economist

"...I do not doubt that it is not only Catholics that this election has moved, delighted and given deep satisfaction to. I can say that I, a Protestant, feel the same. We simply share with our Roman Catholic brothers their joy, their feeling of satisfaction, and their understanding of the great achievement by our countryman... For the first time in the history of the Roman Catholic Church a Slav has become Pope and that Slav is a Pole. This can be expressed not only in the sense of satisfaction to Poles and above all to Catholics in Poland but also in the sense of hope that the influence of the Slav way of thinking and perhaps also Slav emotions will increase in the Roman Catholic Church...

"And now for the hopes which I personally link with the person of Karol Cardinal Wojtyła in his position as Pope John Paul II:

"I have often heard, especially when in Cracow, of the understanding which the present Pope feels for ecumenical problems and the goodwill which he bears to non-Roman Catholics. I think that if, now that he is Pope, he will give some expression of understanding of the ideas of ecumenism, this will have a bearing on a better understanding of ecumenical problems by the Roman Catholic Church in Poland. For in consequence of the fact that the partners in the ecumenical dialogue and in ecumenical coexistence in Poland are on the one hand the mighty Roman Catholic Church and on the other hand a few relatively small Churches, the ecumenical problem in this country is particularly subtle and delicate...

"I feel that Cardinal Karol Wojtyła's very positive attitude towards the renewal movement arouses hope. If Pope John Paul II still has such a positive attitude to the movements of renewal within the Catholic Church, this will help in the animation and consolidation of the religious trend in his Church and in a genuine revival of the Church...

"His resistance to the trappings of Papal worship which we saw during the television broadcast of the celebration of the inauguration of his Pontificate has given me great hope – how he summoned people with a gesture to rise from their knees when they were kneeling before him and how he got up from his throne and went towards the older cardinals to welcome them. I think that this was an expression of his humility and modesty. This was a very kind act and gives me great hope."

Bishop Zdzisław Tranda, the Reformed Church

"As a result of the summoning of a former student of two Polish universities, Cracow and Lublin, a scholar and a Polish poet, to the throne of St. Peter and the Pontificate, Polish culture has certainly received a great honour. This fact may arouse within the atmosphere of the Vatican new animating elements of the nobly understood humanism of our great poets and professors, something of the old Cracow atmosphere, the famed and keen atmosphere with which the ancient Jagiellonian University has always been surrounded.

"I think that the choice of Cardinal Wojtyła as Pope could be the opening of the window of Polish culture, which is so stubbornly disregarded in the West, to the so-called wide world. Such in general are the convictions of Polish opinion."

Jarosław Iwaszkiewicz, writer

"A Pole head of the Catholic Church!... The nature of Polish Catholicism and the Polish Church has been moulded ultimately at the very time of our absence from the stage of world history. The history of the Polish Church in this respect recalls the history of Polish literature. Both the Church and literature have performed the role of a substitute in the life of the nation; both the Church and literature through this have taken on the contents of a substitute; and both the Church and literature have built their prestige in Poland as a result of what is not their most important function. Literature opens men's hearts to the secrets of man and the Church opens men's hearts to the secrets of God. Both the Church and literature in Poland have invigorated the heart instead of opening it. ...The Polish Church is expansive, ritualistic, and collective while in Western Europe and Latin America it tends towards self-examination and individualisation. The Polish Church which for 30 years has co-existed with a socialist system has emphasised tradition in discussions with it; Catholics in Latin America involved in a struggle with totalitarian dictatorships and in the face of extreme poverty are emphasising the revolutionary element of Christian doctrine."

Andrzej Kijowski, literary critic

Twórczość (January 1979): "Not long ago a momentous event startled us which for Poland and not only for Poland is of historical importance. I am thinking of the election of a Pole to the Papal throne. Karol Wojtyła, Pope John Paul II, is now sitting behind the Bronze Gate on the throne of Gregory XVI and Pius XII. To realise the importance of this event, let us imagine what it would have been for Mickiewicz, Słowacki, Krasiński, Norwid, Matejko, Wyspiański, and Stanisław Brzozowski. With what joy they would have received this decision of history.

"With the person of John Paul II Polish culture and history has entered into the orbit of world politics and issues. Karol Wojtyła is seated on his throne armed with the thousand years of European experience of his nation and with the brief albeit concentrated experience of his own life. Wojtyła who was just 19 years of age when the Second World War broke out has personally experienced all the fears and struggles of his generation and knows them. And together with him, seated on the throne in the Vatican is the entire culture of Poland, or to be more exact, the culture of Cracow, the culture of the Jagiellonian University and the culture of the Piast dynasty of our most beloved city. This is a great event indeed."

POPE JOHN PAUL II IN POLAND

"I shall never forget the days which it was granted to me to spend in my beloved Poland. I cherish her in my heart, I wish her constant progress in all areas of spiritual, moral, cultural, social and economic life, and I pray unceasingly for her well-being." This was an excerpt from the message Pope John Paul II sent to the Chairman of the Council of State, Henryk Jabłoński, on his departure from Poland at the end of his pilgrimage tour to the land of his birth.

The visit of John Paul II to Poland became a great emotional experience both for the Pontiff himself and for all those people who gathered to welcome the distinguished guest along the entire route of his journey. The journey began in Warsaw, a city which in all of its long history has never been subdued, a city of peace and the symbol of rebirth from the horrors of war. It continued through Gniezno, the cradle of the Piast dynasty, and Częstochowa, to the Pope's beloved Cracow. It also embraced the Pope's hometown of Wadowice, the Nowy Targ area which is particularly close to him, and Auschwitz, this "Golgotha of the modern world", to use his own words. The solemn Mass celebrated by the Pope with the assistance of priests from among the former prisoners and his homily here were a moving voice of protest against war and a great appeal for peace and the reconciliation of nations.

Many different reasons gave rise to the fact that Pope John Paul II's tour of Poland became an event of international significance. Evidence of this was the exceptionally extensive press coverage of the visit in all continents and also the presence of many of the highest church dignitaries who accompanied His Holiness, as well as the universal interest in the visit not only among the community of 700 million Catholics in the world but also among people of other religious confessions and among non-believers. For the Poles the fact that for the first time in history one of their countrymen – a son of the Polish soil, something which he himself has repeatedly emphasised – had been elected Pope, was further reason for their emotional involvement.

The whole period of John Paul II's visit was attended by genuine Polish hospitality and warmth, both on the part of the highest state officials and the entire population. The Pope gave his thanks for this to Edward Gierek during their memorable meeting at the Belvedere Palace and expressed his respect and esteem to Edward Gierek for the Polish leader's "efforts which are aimed at the common welfare of his countrymen and the due importance of Poland in the international arena".

Pope John Paul II's visit to Poland has entered the history of the Catholic Church both in Poland and the world as an extremely significant chapter in the development of Polish–Vatican and Church–State relations. There is no doubt that this journey has given rise to new important impulses in all areas which contribute to progress in joint dialogue and cooperation, a dialogue, let us add, which has been carried on in Poland in the climate of traditional Polish tolerance and respect for religious freedom, in the spirit of love for a single common homeland of all Poles, regardless of world outlook.

Like a mother one can have only one native country, and for all Poles this is the land between the Rivers Bug and Odra, the Polish People's Republic. This is the native land of the first Polish Pope in history who in June 1979, in the first year of his Pontificate, returned to her as a pilgrim. And it was as a pilgrim that he kissed his beloved native soil upon arrival and departure.

WARSAW, 2 JUNE 1979; Okęcie Airport, 10.07 a.m. Pope John Paul II
arrives in Poland by Alitalia jet to begin his pilgrimage tour of his native country

WARSAW, 2 JUNE; 2 p.m. Edward Gierek, First Secretary of the Polish United Workers' Party, and Henryk Jabłoński, Chairman of the Council of State, receive His Holiness John Paul II and his entourage in the Belvedere Palace

WARSAW, 2–3 JUNE. The Holy Father is warmly welcomed by crowds of Warsaw citizens and pilgrims

WARSAW, 2 JUNE. John Paul II and Stefan Cardinal
Wyszyński, the Primate of Poland, pray at the Tomb of the
Unknown Soldier before the Pope's celebration of Holy Mass in
Victory Square

GNIEZNO, 3–4 JUNE. During his pilgrimage Pope John Paul II visited Gniezno, the city connected with the cult of St. Adalbert, where Poland's first bishopric was established in A.D. 1000

CZĘSTOCHOWA, 4–6 JUNE. At the Shrine of
the Black Madonna at Jasna Góra the Pontiff
celebrated Mass for the faithful from Lower
Silesia, the Opole district, the Lubusz region (5
June) and for pilgrims from Upper Silesia and the
Dąbrowa Basin (6 June), and also took part in the
169th plenary conference of the Polish Episcopate

AUSCHWITZ-BIRKENAU, AFTERNOON OF 7 JUNE. One of the most moving moments during the Pope's pilgrimage – the ceremonies on the site of the former Nazi extermination camp: the Pope praying in front of the Wall of Death, by the International Memorial to the Victims of Fascism, and the memorial mass conducted by John Paul II and priests who were former inmates of Auschwitz

KALWARIA ZEBRZYDOWSKA, 7 JUNE. During an open-air Mass the Pope mentioned his own personal links with this Marian Shrine

WADOWICE, 7 JUNE. The Pope's hometown. John Paul II was baptised in the parish church here in 1920

NOWY TARG, 8 JUNE. The altar, in the style of the traditional architecture of
the Tatra region, in the airfield near Nowy Targ where the Pope gave a homily
for a large congregation including many pilgrims from other countries

CRACOW, EVENING OF 6 JUNE. Warmly
welcomed by the city administration and crowds of
townspeople John Paul II reaches Wawel
Cathedral

CRACOW, 9 JUNE. Among the many places which the Pope visited in his beloved Cracow was the Church of Our Lady with its magnificent altar piece by Wit Stwosz

MOGIŁA, 9 JUNE. At the Cistercian Monastery the Pope meets crowds of pilgrims who have come here to the Sanctuary of the Holy Cross of Jesus

CRACOW, 10 JUNE. On the last day of his stay in Poland John Paul II concelebrated a solemn Mass in honour of St. Stanislaus, Bishop of Cracow, for the many church dignitaries and faithful who were present

Opposite page: Many Poles resident abroad came to Poland to attend celebrations connected with John Paul IÍs visit

Cracow, 10 June; 4.55 p.m. His Holiness John
Paul II leaves for Rome aboard the plane of the
Polish airlines LOT

Production editor:
Wiesław Pyszka

Colour photographs by
S. Jabłońska, K. Kamiński (PAI), A. Kossobudzki-Orłowski, W. Kryński, B. Łopieński, L. Łożyński,
J. Morek (PAI), W. Ochnio (PAI), T. Prażmowski, J. Rosikoń, B. Różyc (PAI), Ruckgaber,
T. Sumiński, Z. Szczęsny, Z. Wdowiński, A. Zborski and L. Zielaskowski (PAI)

Cover photograph by
A. Kossobudzki-Orłowski

Black-and-white photographs by
C. Grodzki, J. Hałasa, M. Kolasa, A. Kossobudzki-Orłowski, E. Lewandowska, M. Łoziński,
J. Morek, A. Pacyga, A. Ruckgaber and Z. Szczęsny, and by Photoservice of the Polish Interpress
Agency, *Hejnał Mariacki* and *Za i Przeciw*

This book appears also in Polish

PRINTED IN YUGOSLAVIA, GORENJSKI TISK, KRANJ